N3

Coming Together

Book 1

Integrating Math and Language

Julie Rumi Iwamoto

Prentice Hall Regents
Englewood Cliffs, New Jersey 07632

Acquistions Editor: *Nancy Leonhardt*
Director of Production and Manufacturing: *David Riccardi*
Editorial Production/Design Manager: *Dominick Mosco*
Electronic/production supervision and interior design: *Noël Vreeland Carter*
Page Composition: *Ken Liao*
Production Coordinator: *Ray Keating*
Cover Coordinator: *Merle Krumper*

Illustrations: *Don Martinetti*
Cover Designer: *Mike Fender*

Printed in the United States of America

10   9   8   7   6   5

ISBN 0-13-210451-2

Prentice-Hall International (UK) Limited, London
Prentice-Hall of Australia Pty. Limited, Sydney
Prentice-Hall Canada Inc., Toronto
Prentice-Hall Hispanoamericana, S.A., Mexico
Prentice-Hall of India Private Limited, New Delhi
Prentice-Hall of Japan, Inc., Tokyo
Simon & Schuster Asia Pte. Ltd., Singapore
Editora Prentice-Hall do Brasil, Ltda., Rio de Janeiro

For my brother Koki

Contents

Unit 4   Operations with Decimal Numbers   135

Preface

Coming Together Book 1 is written for teachers who have little or no experience in teaching math to limited English speaking students. It merges the teaching of math with English language acquisition exercises specifically related to mathematical concepts and terminology. For that reason, the language contained in the book is sheltered: in place of complex sentences and lengthy explanations, sentences are written in the present tense, simple, with extensive use of examples and illustrations. Vocabulary exercises are found in each chapter and definitions, when necessary, are kept short. Word problems in each chapter are written around a central theme that is appropriate to secondary students and reflective of real life, practical, situations (high school activities, working part-time, budgeting, and shopping, among other topics). Features of the book include:

1. listening exercises where the students identify words or phrases that they hear the teacher say aloud,
2. speaking exercises where the students practice pronouncing cardinal and ordinal numbers, decimal numbers, and mathematical phrases, along with a list of vocabulary words to be discussed orally with the teacher,
3. written exercises where the students write into words numbers, decimals, and mathematical phrases and terms,
4. reading passages where students read dialogues or situations that incorporate vocabulary specific to math,
5. a list of vocabulary words for each chapter as well as a glossary at the end of each unit,
6. and finally, chapter review exercises at the end of each chapter.

Coming Together Book 1 covers cardinal and ordinal numbers, the operations of addition, subtraction, multiplication, division, number theory, and decimals. *Coming Together Book 2* covers fractions, ratios, percents, operations with positive and negative integers, and an introduction to geometry. Although these books are written with the limited English speaker in mind, they are by no means confined to them. Students reading below grade level will also benefit from these books, as language and vocabulary are carefully structured in each chapter.

As a math teacher for the past several years to limited English speaking students, I have realized the need for a book that will enable these students to learn math while at the same time, learn the language necessary to master the subject. It is my hope that this book will make learning math a little less frustrating for all limited English speaking students as well as for their teachers.

Acknowledgments

I would like to thank my children, Filip and Sayuri, and my mother, all who have been very encouraging and patient throughout this endeavor. And I would especially like to thank my father, Koya Iwamoto, my first math teacher, for his critical help and guidance throughout the writing of this book and for sharing with me his love for mathematics.

UNIT 1

Base Ten Number System

1 2 3 4 5 6 7 8 9 0 π

1234567890⌐

1234567890⊀

1234567890 +

1234567890 √

0123456789 ÷

√0987654321

+0987654321

⊀0987654321

⌐0987654321

π0987654321

1

1 Reading and Saying Cardinal Numbers

1-1 Cardinal Numbers

We count with **cardinal numbers**. We use cardinal numbers to answer the question, *"How many?"*

0 – zero	7 – seven	14 – fourteen
1 – one	8 – eight	15 – fifteen
2 – two	9 – nine	16 – sixteen
3 – three	10 – ten	17 – seventeen
4 – four	11 – eleven	18 – eighteen
5 – five	12 – twelve	19 – nineteen
6 – six	13 – thirteen	20 – twenty

21 – twenty-one, (twenty-two, twenty-three, twenty-four, twenty-five, twenty-six, twenty-seven, twenty-eight, twenty-nine)

30 – thirty, (thirty-one, thirty-two, . . .)

40 – forty, (fifty, sixty, seventy, eighty, ninety)

100 – one hundred, (one hundred one, one hundred two, . . .)

200 – two hundred, (three hundred, four hundred, . . .)

1,000 – one thousand, (one thousand one, one thousand two, . . .)

2,000 – two thousand, (three thousand, four thousand, . . .)

10,000 – ten thousand, (twenty thousand, thirty thousand, . . .)

100,000 – one hundred thousand, (two hundred thousand, three hundred thousand, . . .)

1,000,000 – one million, (two million, three million, . . .)

1,000,000,000 – one billion, (two billion, three billion, . . .)

DEFINITION: Digit

The numbers 0, 1, 2, 3, 4, 5, 6, 7, 8, 9, have one *digit*.
The numbers 10, 11, 12, 13, . . ., 99 have two *digits*.
The numbers 100, 101, 102, 103, . . ., 999 have three *digits*.
The numbers 1,000, 1,001, 1,002, . . ., 9,999 have four *digits*.

A **digit** is any of the numbers 0, 1, 2, 3, 4, 5, 6, 7, 8, 9.

How many digits does the number 56 have? ____

How many digits does the number 1,257 have? ____

How many digits does the number 34,589 have? ____

In a *one-digit* number, we write a digit in the

$$
\begin{array}{c}
\underline{} \\
\uparrow \\
\text{ones' place}
\end{array}
\qquad
\begin{array}{c}
\underline{8} \\
\uparrow \\
(8 \times 1) = 8
\end{array}
$$

In a *two-digit* number, we write the two digits in the

$$
\begin{array}{c}
\underline{}\ \underline{} \\
\uparrow\ \uparrow \\
\end{array}
$$

ones' place and
tens' place

$$
\begin{array}{c}
\underline{2}\ \underline{8} \\
\uparrow\ \uparrow \\
(8 \times 1) = 8 \\
(2 \times 10) = 20 \\
20 + 8 = 28
\end{array}
$$

In a *three-digit* number, we write the three digits in the

ones' place
tens' place, and
hundreds' place

$$
\begin{array}{c}
\underline{3}\ \underline{2}\ \underline{8} \\
\uparrow\ \uparrow\ \uparrow \\
(8 \times 1) = 8 \\
(2 \times 10) = 20 \\
(3 \times 100) = 300 \\
300 + 20 + 8 = 328
\end{array}
$$

In a *four-digit* number, we write the four digits in the

ones' place
tens' place,
hundreds' place, and
thousands' place

$$
\begin{array}{c}
\underline{7}\ \underline{3}\ \underline{2}\ \underline{8} \\
\uparrow\ \uparrow\ \uparrow\ \uparrow \\
(8 \times 1) = 8 \\
(2 \times 10) = 20 \\
(3 \times 100) = 300 \\
(7 \times 1,000) = 7,000 \\
7,000 + 300 + 20 + 8 = 7,328
\end{array}
$$

Base Ten Numeration System

Place Names from Ones' to Billions':

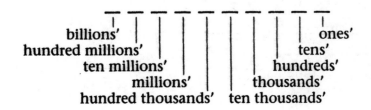

billions'
hundred millions'
ten millions'
millions'
hundred thousands'   ten thousands'
thousands'
hundreds'
tens'
ones'

In numbers with more than three digits, we write a **comma** "," between certain digits. This helps us read the number correctly.

Example:

Begin at the ones' place and count three digits to the left. ←

<pre>
2 , 4 7 5   3 , 2 5 6 , 4 7 8
    ↑ 3 digits   ↑ 3 digits ↑ 3 digits
    | | |
  comma   comma   comma
</pre>

Write a comma before the: thousands' place,
millions' place, and
billions' place.

Exercise 1-A

Rewrite the numbers with *commas*.

1. 34566	4. 25478	7. 1839984765	10. 4903944
2. 35879800	5. 1569385	8. 12986	11. 70004301
3. 1243	6. 48765321	9. 3678	12. 152946450710

What is the place name of the <u>underlined</u> digit?

13. 8<u>9</u> *ones'*	16. 38,2<u>9</u>6	19. 1<u>2</u>5,746,150
14. <u>1</u>94	17. 42<u>9</u>,126	20. <u>1</u>1,244
15. 6,<u>7</u>24	18. 7,01<u>2</u>	21. 21<u>5</u>,494,199

22. 6<u>4</u>,640
23. 11,<u>1</u>11,211
24. 234,5<u>67</u>

25. <u>7</u>,345,879
26. 1<u>2</u>3,456
27. 34,3<u>6</u>7

28. 3<u>6</u>7,119,026
29. 90,08<u>0</u>
30. <u>9</u>,824,674,113

Copy *all* the numbers with:

31. 6 in the *tens'* place:
   26   62   56   68   36
   Answer: 62, 68

32. 9 in the *ones'* place:
   89   98   79   95   94

33. 8 in the *tens'* place:
   78   89   18   82   88

34. 5 in the *hundreds'* place:
   152   125   345   546

35. 2 in the *ones'* place:
   27   72   52   23   12

36. 3 in the *thousands'* place:
   4,356   3,446   5,432   2,345

37. 1 in the *tens'* place:
   177   712   8,123   13   21

38. 2 in the *ones'* place:
   28   82   423   9,432   12

39. 4 in the *hundreds'* place:
   345   564   4,567   3,478   432

40. 3 in the *hundred thousands'* place:
   366,578   3,467,112
   254,533,679   1,348,990

41. 9 in the *ten thousands'* place:
   19,877   98,399   198,734   195,877

42. 5 in the *millions'* place:
   45,986,433   4,678,445
   153,345,672   65,456,788

1-4 How Do You Say ... the Numbers?

For all 3-digit numbers, say *hundred* after the hundreds' digit:

<u>2 4 3</u>

two *hundred* forty-three

<u>1 0 6</u>

one *hundred* six

For all 4-, 5-, and 6- digit numbers, say *thousand* after the thousands' digit or at the comma:

1 , <u>2 1 4</u>

one   two hundred
thousand,   fourteen

<u>3 0 4</u> , <u>9 1 7</u>

three hundred   nine hundred
four *thousand,*   seventeen

For all 7-, 8-, and 9- digit numbers, say *million* after the millions' digit and *thousand* after the thousands' digit:

<u>4 2 1</u> , <u>6 0 4</u> , <u>0 9 0</u>

four hundred   six hundred   ninety
twenty-one   four
million,   *thousand,*

For all 10-, 11-, and 12-digit numbers, say *billion*, *million*, and *thousand* after the billions', millions', and thousands' digits or at all three commas:

$$2 \; , \; 1 \; 0 \; 3 \; , \; 2 \; 1 \; 6 \; , \; 1 \; 5 \; 6$$

two billion,	one hundred three million,	two hundred sixteen thousand,	one hundred fifty-six

---

Exercise 1-B

Say these numbers aloud.

1. 27	10. 13	19. 19	28. 3,010
2. 12	11. 57	20. 101	29. 2,001
3. 38	12. 93	21. 234	30. 10,113
4. 55	13. 19	22. 769	31. 85,200
5. 14	14. 55	23. 500	32. 96,002
6. 11	15. 20	24. 927	33. 75,414
7. 0	16. 42	25. 812	34. 125,308
8. 40	17. 88	26. 1,324	35. 2,670,008
9. 79	18. 90	27. 6,719	36. 6,500,013

LISTEN! Saying and Reading Numbers

Your teacher will read numbers aloud. Listen. Then on your own paper, write the letter that appears next to the number you hear.

1. a. 29 b. 290 c. 129	4. a. 999 b. 919 c. 990	7. a. 6,190,260 b. 6,190,260,000 c. 6,119,260	10. a. 8,600,095 b. 8,695,000 c. 8,006,095
2. a. 40 b. 14 c. 43	5. a. 3,150 b. 3,150,000 c. 3,115	8. a. 107,003 b. 107,030 c. 107,300	11. a. 600,009 b. 609,000 c. 600,900
3. a. 315 b. 350 c. 3,500	6. a. 426,030 b. 426,300 c. 426,013	9. a. 5,315,000 b. 5,300,000 c. 5,350,000	12. a. 40,000,550 b. 14,550,000 c. 14,000,055

Mr. Wilson: How much is that sofa?

Mr. Green: It's one hundred and fifty dollars.

Mr. Wilson: How old is that sofa?

Mr. Green: It's two years old.

Mr. Wilson: How much is the television set?

Mr. Green: It's seventy dollars.

Mr. Wilson: And the refrigerator?

Mr. Green: It's eighty-nine dollars.

Mr. Wilson: I see. How about that rug?

Mr. Green: Oh, it's very old. It's three hundred fifteen years old and it's seven hundred seventy dollars.

Mr. Wilson: Okay. I'll take everything!

1. The refrigerator costs
   a. $18   b. $98   c. $89   d. $809

2. The sofa is
   a. 1 years old   b. 2 years old   c. 20 years old   d. 22 years old

3. The sofa costs
   a. $150   b. $115   c. $105   d. $501

4. The television set costs
   a. $17   b. $700   c. $70   d. $7

5. The rug is
   a. 350 years old b. 305 years old c. 355 years old d. 315 years old

---

Exercise 1-D

Write the cardinal numbers in English.

1. 10   *ten*   3. 12   5. 90   7. 0
2. 13   4. 19   6. 40   8. 11

9. 33	12. 88	15. 207	18. 12,945
10. 87	13. 102	16. 1,980	19. 1,345,009
11. 77	14. 158	17. 2,012	20. 13,405,090

Write the number.

21. fifty *50*

22. sixty-four

23. eleven thousand

24. one thousand six

25. six hundred ten

26. forty-five hundred

27. nine thousand, eleven

28. three thousand, thirty-seven

29. eighty-seven

30. fifty-four

31. four hundred five thousand, nine hundred nineteen

32. one million, six hundred thousand

33. two hundred fifty thousand, three

34. sixteen million, nine hundred fifty thousand, four hundred fourteen

35. three hundred eleven thousand, nine hundred fourteen

36. twenty-three thousand, two hundred two

37. seventeen thousand, sixty

38. three million, eight hundred ninety thousand, five hundred twenty-nine

39. eight billion, seventy-seven thousand, sixteen

40. seventy-five hundred

Exercise 1-E

Find *16* numbers below that are spelled correctly. Copy those numbers onto your own paper.

nineteen	twenty-one	six hundred	seventy
one	eighty	eigth	fiveteen
eleven	one hundrad	twelve	thurty
foure	fifteen	three	two tausend
twenty	too	fourty	ninty
nine	cero	seventy-five	seben
seventeen	forty	fifty-eight	six milion

Write the matching letter next to the number.

1. 960   _a_   a. nine hundred forty-one

2. 7,432   ___   b. seven hundred forty-three

3. 967   ___   c. seven thousand, four hundred thirty-two

4. 9,670   ___   d. nine hundred sixty-seven

8

5. 743 ___ e. nine thousand, four hundred sixty

6. 94,603 ___ f. nine thousand, six hundred seventy

7. 941 ___ g. nine hundred sixty

8. 44,267 ___ h. nine thousand, four hundred one

9. 9,460 ___ i. nine thousand, four hundred ten

10. 9,410 ___ j. ninety four thousand, six hundred three

11. 9,401 ___ k. forty-four thousand, two hundred sixty-seven

---

VOCABULARY: Numbers from Small to Large

In the following group of numbers:

20, 6, 12, 3, 14, 15, 8, 22

3 is the *smallest* number.

22 is the *largest* or *greatest* number.

8 is the *largest* one-digit number.

12 is the *smallest* two-digit number.

Example:

Write the numbers, **in order,** *from smallest to largest.*

9, 6, 4, 2, 11, 7
Answer: 2, 4, 6, 7, 9, 11

Exercise 1-F

Answer each question with numbers.

1. Write 4 one-digit numbers.

2. Write 4 two-digit numbers.

3. Write 4 three-digit numbers.

4. In this group of numbers: 8, 24, 11, 3, 12, 16, 2, 6, 13
   a. Which number is the greatest or largest?
   b. Which number is the smallest?
   c. What is the smallest two-digit number?
   d. What is the largest one-digit number?

5. Of *all* the cardinal numbers (0, 1, 2, 3, . . ., infinity):
   a. What is the smallest one-digit number?
   b. What is the greatest one-digit number?
   c. What is the smallest two-digit number?
   d. What is the greatest two-digit number?
   e. What is the smallest three-digit number?
   f. What is the greatest three-digit number?

6. Write the following numbers in order, from small to large.

2,344	2,433	2,044	2,244
2,342	2,004	2,343	2,400
2,304	2,440	2,330	2,432
2,240	2,043	2,204	2,040

LET'S TALK ABOUT ...

1. digit	7. least	13. hundreds' place
2. comma	8. value	14. thousands' place
3. place	9. number	15. ten thousands' place
4. largest	10. cardinal	16. hundred thousands' place
5. greatest	11. ones' place	17. millions' place
6. smallest	12. tens' place	18. ten millions' place

Write the cardinal numbers in English.

1. 11	3. 15	5. 8	7. 130	9. 3,607
2. 0	4. 12	6. 40	8. 289	10. 57,289

Write the numbers.

11. three hundred sixteen

12. four thousand two

13. five hundred ten thousand, six hundred eleven

14. two million, three hundred seventy thousand, nine hundred fifteen

Write the place names of the underlined number.

15. 2<u>4</u>5	17. <u>3</u>,578	19. 1<u>9</u>6,590	21. <u>4</u>99
16. 3<u>1</u>	18. <u>2</u>45,792	20. <u>1</u>,284,765	22. <u>2</u>3,598,743

Look at the following numbers.

127,938	7,146,783	129
394,398	6,258	11,404
2,278,500	637,146,783	181,328,934

Copy the number with:

23. 9 in the ones' place

24. 4 in the hundreds' place

25. 2 in the hundred thousands' place

26. 5 in the ten's place

27. 7 in the thousands' place

28. 9 in the ten thousands' place

29. 1 in the millions' place

30. 3 in the ten millions' place

2 | Reading and Saying Ordinal Numbers

2-1 | Ordinal Numbers

When we talk about **order**, we use **ordinal numbers**:

1st	first	11th	eleventh	21st	twenty-first
2nd	second	12th	twelfth	22nd	twenty-second
3rd	third	13th	thirteenth	23rd	twenty-third
4th	fourth	14th	fourteenth	30th	thirtieth
5th	fifth	15th	fifteenth	40th	fortieth
6th	sixth	16th	sixteenth	50th	fiftieth
7th	seventh	17th	seventeenth	60th	sixtieth
8th	eighth	18th	eighteenth	70th	seventieth
9th	ninth	19th	nineteenth	80th	eightieth
10th	tenth	20th	twentieth	90th	ninetieth

100th	one hundredth, (one hundred-first, one hundred-second, . . .)
1,000th	one thousandth, (two thousandths, three thousandths, . . .)
1,000,000th	one millionth, (two millionths, three millionths, . . .)

Write an ordinal number for each cardinal number.

1. 4 *4th*	9. 90	17. 16
2. 9	10. 1	18. 22
3. 2	11. 3	19. 31
4. 7	12. 102	20. 19
5. 11	13. 70	21. 60
6. 5	14. 61	22. 42
7. 33	15. 53	23. 75
8. 45	16. 99	24. 203

Say these numbers aloud.

25. 10th	30. 13th	35. 80th	40. 15th
26. 1st	31. 43rd	36. 8th	41. 70th
27. 32nd	32. 19th	37. 17th	42. 91st
28. 25th	33. 40th	38. 32nd	43. 83rd
29. 50th	34. 77th	39. 100th	44. 93rd

Write the ordinal numbers in English.

45. 6th *sixth*	53. 40th	61. 2,000th
46. 19th	54. 8th	62. 81st
47. 1st	55. 29th	63. 104th
48. 5th	56. 75th	64. 203rd
49. 90th	57. 50th	65. 77th
50. 12th	58. 4th	66. 88th
51. 42nd	59. 20th	67. 1,001st
52. 3rd	60. 100th	68. 24th

Read the following words.

Homework by magic, that is my scheme.

1. What is the third word of the line?

2. What is the last word of the line?

3. What is the first word of the line?

4. What are the first three words of the line?

5. What is the fourth word of the line?

Read the following poem.

HOMEWORK BY MAGIC

Homework by magic, that is my scheme.
It's homework by magic; a wonderful dream.
Just a trip to the Homework Arcade,
The cost of a quarter and I'd have it all made.
Drop in the coin, slide in the paper
And trouble is gone as if it were vapor.
As fast as can be "what's ten minus three?"
Oh, it must equal four.
Equal four!?
More answers like that and my grades will be poor!

Noël Vreeland Carter*

_____

* By permission of the author

6. What is the second word of the second line?

7. What is the second word of the fourth line?

8. What is the fourth word of the fifth line?

9. What are the last four words of the eighth line?

10. What are the last three words of the seventh line?

11. What are the third and fourth words of the sixth line?

12. What is the second word of the seventh line?

13. What is the eighth word of the seventh line?

14. What is the last word of the poem?

SPEAKING UP! Saying and Reading Numbers

Look at the program card that follows. Your teacher will ask you questions about the card. Answer aloud.

Mora	Ricky	10	10-18-75	9-21-92
Last Name	First	Grade	Birthdate	Date

Per.	Room	Class Title	Teacher
1	104	English 10	Brown
2	323	Algebra 1	Williams
3	121	U.S. History	Garcia
4	205	Biology	Kodama
5	gym	Physical Education	Stein
6	313	Art	Kato

This is Robin's calendar. She has many things to do. Look at the calendar and complete the sentences.

Sunday	Monday	Tuesday	Wednesday	Thursday	Friday	Saturday
	1 Go to bank $	2	3 Letter to M.	4	5 Tennis with R.	6
7	8 See Doctor Z.	9	10 J's birthday	11	12 Music lesson ♪ 4:00	13
14	15 Go to library	16 Dentist 3:00	17	18 Lunch with S.	19	20 Hair appointment
21	22	23	24 Visit Mother	25	26	27 Baseball game!
28 Wash car	29	30	31 Pay rent!!!			

1. What will Robin do on Monday, the fifteenth?
2. On the twenty-seventh, there is a _____.
3. On the twenty-fourth, Robin will _____.
4. What will Robin do on the first day of the month?

Answer with *cardinal* numbers. Write all numbers in English.

5. There are _____ days in this month.
6. There are _____ days in a week.
7. There are _____ Wednesdays in this month.
8. There are _____ Fridays in this month.

Answer with *ordinal* numbers. Write all numbers in English.

9. Look at the first week. The month begins on Monday, the _____.

10. On the _____ day of the month, Robin has a "music lesson" at 4:00.

11. Look at the second week. Wednesday is the _____ day of the month.

12. Robin will "pay rent" on the _____ day of the month.

13. She will play "tennis with R." on Friday, the _____.

14. On Sunday, the _____, Robin will "wash car."

15. Robin has a "hair appointment" on Saturday, the _____.

16. This calendar shows that Thursday is the _____ day of the week.

17. On the _____ day of the month, Robin will "see Doctor Z."

18. Robin will write a "letter to M." on the _____ day of the month.

2-2 | How Do You Say ... the Dates?

We write dates in this order:

Month – Day – Year

May 4, 1990
5/4/90
5-4-90

We use cardinal and ordinal numbers when we read or say dates:

May 4, 1990
We say: "May fourth, nineteen ninety"

5/4/90
We say: "five, four, ninety"

Exercise 2-D

Practice saying these dates aloud.

1. June 2, 1988
2. February 11, 1975
3. December 25, 1991
4. 1/7/87

5. June 8, 1847
6. January 1, 1984
7. 7/11/66
8. March 17, 1981

9. May 3, 1909
10. November 21, 1888
11. July 4, 1776
12. 8/29/71

Look at Annabell's photos below and on page 19. They are *not* in order. Write the dates in correct *order* below, from earliest to latest.

1. *4/7/38—Annabell born*   3.   5.
2.   4.   6.

7-11-63
To Europe!

4-1-66
Joey's Birthday!

May 3, 1970
To California!

July 7, 1963
Just Married!

April 1, 1965
Joey is born!

8/11/70
Family Picnic!

7.

8.

9.

10.

11.

12.

7-5-62
To Italy!

3/19/'65
Our new car!

9-11-66
Matilde is born!

6/20/60
My diploma!

4-7-38
Annabell is born!

Feb. 15, 1962
To New York!

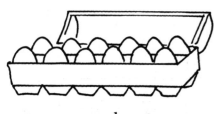

one dozen

double

pair

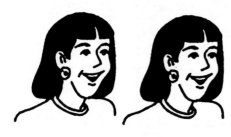

twins

couple

triplets

single

half dozen

Tina works in Flora's Flower Shop. She takes orders for flowers and sends the flowers to the customers.

Tina: Flora, here is an order for a dozen roses for Mr. and Mrs. Richardson. They are parents of twin girls!

Flora: That's wonderful!

Tina: Oh, and here is an order to send a couple of green plants to Mrs. Carl. She is in the hospital.

Flora: All right. Tina, I have a pair of tickets to the circus. Do you want them?

Tina: Sure! I'll ask Gerald if he wants to go with me. He is single and has some time, I think. Flora, how much are roses now?

Flora: Roses are $8.00 for a half dozen. The price of roses has doubled in 4 years!

Tina: So that's $16.00 for a dozen roses.

Flora: That's right! Tina, I must hurry home! My cat Daisy had kittens last night! Quadruplets! My house is full of cats!

Tina: Okay, Flora. See you tomorrow! And thanks for the tickets!

Read the dialogue, **Flora's Flower Shop**, then answer the questions.

  1. How many baby girls do Mr. and Mrs. Richardson have?

  2. How many roses did Tina send to Mr. and Mrs. Richardson?

  3. How many green plants go to Mrs. Carl?

  4. Is Gerald married?

  5. How many circus tickets did Flora give to Tina?

  6. How much are a dozen roses?

  7. For $8.00, how many roses can you buy?

  8. How much were a half-dozen roses 4 years ago?

  9. How many roses can you get for $16.00?

  10. How many kittens did Daisy have last night?

1. order
2. ordinal
3. first
4. second
5. third
6. fourth
7. fifth
8. eighth
9. ninth
10. twelfth
11. twentieth
12. single
13. pair
14. couple
15. twins
16. double
17. triple
18. dozen
19. quadruple
20. triplets
21. half-dozen

Write the ordinal numbers in English.

1. 5th
2. 9th
3. 8th
4. 12th
5. 21st
6. 33rd
7. 11th
8. 200th
9. 15th
10. 92nd

Write the ordinal numbers.

11. first
12. second
13. third
14. tenth
15. forty-third
16. three hundred sixty- second
17. one thousandth
18. sixtieth
19. nineteenth
20. seventy-fifth

Copy the following 12 boxes onto your own paper.

☐ ☐ ☐ ☐ ☐ ☐ ☐ ☐ ☐ ☐ ☐ ☐

21. Write an "X" in the fourth box.

22. Write a "Y" in the eighth box.

23. Write an "M" in the third box.

24. Write an "O" in the eleventh box.

25. Write an "A" in the first box.

26. Write an "L" in the fifth box.

27. Write a "B" in the tenth box.

28. Write a "C" in the twelfth box.

29. Write a "T" in the second box.

30. Write an "S" in the sixth box.

31. Write a "J" in the ninth box.

32. Write a "P" in the seventh box.

3   Rounding Off Numbers

3-1   Round Numbers

What is a round number? Look at the following examples:

40			43
10			15
350			345
5,000	All of these are	All of these are not	5,467
70	round numbers	round numbers	78
220			228
7,500			7,598
870			871

DEFINITION: Round Number

A **round number** is a number that is written with *zero* as the last digit.

Example:

20
310

A *round number* may have more than one zero:

Example:

200
31,000

Why do you think we call these *round* numbers?

Exercise 3-A

Which numbers are *round* numbers?

1. 450	6. 325	11. 4,909
2. 678	7. 567	12. 13
3. 324	8. 45,900	13. 60,001
4. 540	9. 1,000	14. 30
5. 2,400	10. 500	15. 56,677

To **round off** a number means to change a number to a round number. We can round off a number to the tens' place, hundreds' place, thousands' place, and so on:

5,231 rounds off to 5,230 (tens' place)
5,200 (hundreds' place)
5,000 (thousands' place)

Example:

We *round off* the number 23 to the *tens'* place → 20.
We *round off* the number 276 to the *hundreds'* place → 300.
We *round off* the number 6,437 to the *thousands'* place → 6,000.

DEFINITION: Number Line

This is a **number line**:

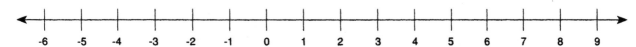

The number line continues to the right → and it continues to the left ←. There is no end because it is *infinite*. The numbers on the left are *less than* the numbers on the right. The numbers on the right are *greater than* the numbers on the left:

5 is less than 6.
8 is greater than 7.

3-2 Rounding Off Numbers

Look at the following number line:

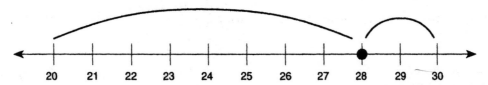

This part of the number line has numbers from 20 to 30. The number 28 is between the round numbers 20 and 30. 28 is closer to 30, so we can *round off* 28 to 30:

28 → 30

Is the number 23 closer to 20 or 30? 23 is closer to 20, so we can *round off* 23 to 20:

23 → 20

Exercise 3-B

Round off to the closer round number 10 or 20.

1. 18 →   3. 13 →   5. 11 → .   7. 19 →
2. 12 →   4. 16 →   6. 14 →   8. 17 →

What about the number 15? It is exactly in the *middle*, between the round numbers 10 and 20. Do we round to 10 or 20?

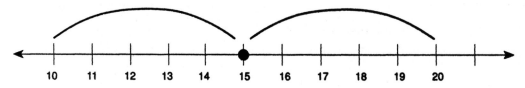

Rule:

When the number is exactly in the middle of two round numbers, always round off to the *greater* round number.

15 → 20

Exercise 3-C

Round off to 30 or 40.

1. 33 →   4. 39 →
2. 36 →   5. 31 →
3. 35 →   6. 37 →

Round off to 80 or 90.

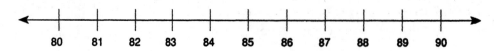

7. 84 →   10. 85 →
8. 88 →   11. 89 →
9. 87 →   12. 82 →

Round off to 100 or 200.

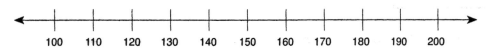

13. 180 →   18. 151 →   23. 130 →

14. 110 →   19. 149 →   24. 199 →

15. 175 →   20. 124 →   25. 140 →

16. 105 →   21. 195 →   26. 177 →

17. 150 →   22. 167 →   27. 112 →

Round off to 200 or 300.

28. 286 →   32. 250 →   36. 233 →

29. 225 →   33. 244 →   37. 261 →

30. 205 →   34. 278 →   38. 283 →

31. 269 →   35. 249 →   39. 210 →

3-3 Rounding Off to Tens' Place

Example:

*Round off the number 123 to the nearest **tens' place**.*

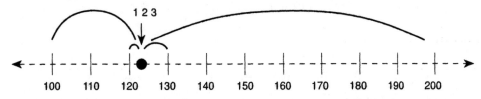

123 is between the round numbers 120 and 130. 123 is also between the round numbers 100 and 200.

We can round off 123 to the nearest tens' place (120), *or* we can round off 123 to the nearest hundreds' place (100).

To round off 123 to the nearest *tens'* place, *underline* the tens' place digit and look at the number to the right.

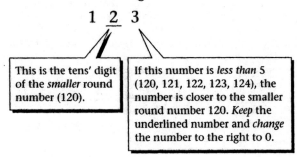

1 <u>2</u> 3

This is the tens' digit of the *smaller* round number (120).

If this number is *less than* 5 (120, 121, 122, 123, 124), the number is closer to the smaller round number 120. *Keep* the underlined number and *change* the number to the right to 0.

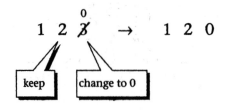

Answer: 1 2 3 → 1 2 0

Example:

Round off 156 to the nearest tens' place: Underline the tens' place digit and look at the number to right.

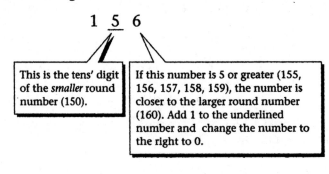

1 5 6

This is the tens' digit of the *smaller* round number (150).

If this number is 5 or greater (155, 156, 157, 158, 159), the number is closer to the larger round number (160). Add 1 to the underlined number and change the number to the right to 0.

1 5̸ 6̸ → 1 6 0

5 + 1 = 6 | change to 0

Answer: 1 5 6 → 1 6 0

Example:

Round off 196 to the nearest tens' place.

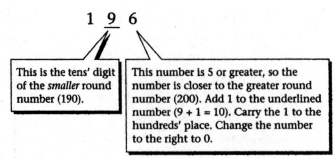

1 9 6

This is the tens' digit of the *smaller* round number (190).

This number is 5 or greater, so the number is closer to the greater round number (200). Add 1 to the underlined number (9 + 1 = 10). Carry the 1 to the hundreds' place. Change the number to the right to 0.

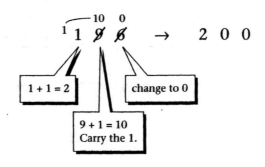

$$\overset{\overset{\displaystyle 10 \quad 0}{\big\downarrow}}{^1 1 \; \cancel{9} \; \cancel{6}} \quad \rightarrow \quad 2 \; 0 \; 0$$

1 + 1 = 2

change to 0

9 + 1 = 10
Carry the 1.

Answer: 1 9 6 → 2 0 0

Rule for Rounding Off

Underline the number. Look at the number to the right.

If the number to the right is less than 5:

0
1
2
3
4

Keep the underlined number.
Change all numbers to the right to zeroes.

If the number to the right is 5 or greater:

5
6
7
8
9

Add 1 to the underlined number.
Change all numbers to the right to zeroes.

Exercise 3-D

Round off each number to the nearest tens' place.

1. 24	11. 21	21. 957
2. 59	12. 33	22. 806
3. 73	13. 85	23. 4,235
4. 89	14. 39	24. 1,455
5. 15	15. 11	25. 824
6. 65	16. 132	26. 23,493
7. 91	17. 249	27. 711
8. 78	18. 895	28. 6,201
9. 99	19. 451	29. 15,394
10. 18	20. 1,321	30. 2,035

Example:

Round off the number 357 to the nearest hundreds' place.

Underline the hundreds' place digit and look at the number to the right.

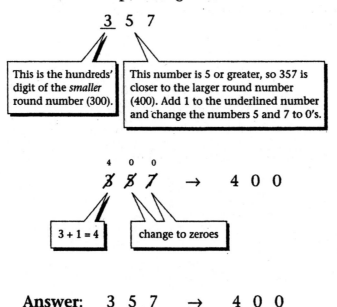

$$3\ 5\ 7$$

This is the hundreds' digit of the *smaller* round number (300).

This number is 5 or greater, so 357 is closer to the larger round number (400). Add 1 to the underlined number and change the numbers 5 and 7 to 0's.

$$\overset{4\quad 0\quad 0}{\cancel{3}\ \cancel{5}\ \cancel{7}} \rightarrow 4\ 0\ 0$$

3 + 1 = 4   change to zeroes

Answer: 3 5 7 → 4 0 0

Example:

Round off the number 983 to the nearest hundreds' place.

Underline the hundreds' place digit and look at the digit to the right.

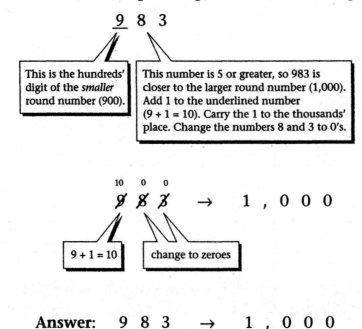

$$9\ 8\ 3$$

This is the hundreds' digit of the *smaller* round number (900).

This number is 5 or greater, so 983 is closer to the larger round number (1,000). Add 1 to the underlined number (9 + 1 = 10). Carry the 1 to the thousands' place. Change the numbers 8 and 3 to 0's.

$$\overset{10\quad 0\quad 0}{\cancel{9}\ \cancel{8}\ \cancel{3}} \rightarrow 1\ ,\ 0\ 0\ 0$$

9 + 1 = 10   change to zeroes

Answer: 9 8 3 → 1 , 0 0 0

Example:

Round off 32,489 to the nearest thousands' place.

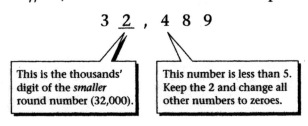

3 2 , 4 8 9

| This is the thousands' digit of the *smaller* round number (32,000). | This number is less than 5. Keep the 2 and change all other numbers to zeroes. |

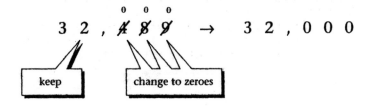

3 2 , 4̶ 8̶ 9̶ → 3 2 , 0 0 0

keep   change to zeroes

Answer: 3 2 , 4 8 9   →   3 2 , 0 0 0

Exercise 3-E

Round off each number to the nearest *hundreds'* place.

1. 124	6. 156	11. 913	16. 2,395
2. 387	7. 989	12. 999	17. 8,941
3. 506	8. 321	13. 315	18. 7,056
4. 450	9. 651	14. 849	19. 21,994
5. 872	10. 721	15. 1,429	20. 3,651

Round off each number to the nearest *thousands'* place.

21. 3,455	26. 4,355	31. 24,937	36. 32,941
22. 6,899	27. 25,678	32. 127,095	37. 254,953
23. 1,237	28. 2,905	33. 11,277	38. 365,019
24. 6,987	29. 34,439	34. 29,821	39. 240,677
25. 7,500	30. 67,539	35. 956,499	40. 2,346,771

3-5 Estimation

When we **estimate** or **approximate**, we are really *rounding off*. We want to know *about how much* or *about how many*. An estimate or approximation is *usually not* an exact amount.

Example:

> *Isabel paid $53 for a new dress. She told her mother that she paid about $50.*
> *She rounded off $53 to the nearest tens' (or nearest ten dollars).*

$$\$53 \approx \$50$$

The symbol $\approx$ means *is approximately*.

Example:

> *The Tigers basketball team scored 78 points, 51 points, and 66 points in three*
> *games. Approximate the total points to the nearest **tens'** place.*

$$78 \approx 80$$
$$51 \approx 50$$
$$\underline{66 \approx 70}$$

Total: 200 points

They scored *approximately* 200 points in 3 games.

Exercise 3-F

Estimate or approximate each answer.

1. (*to the tens' place*) Matilde drove 32 miles on Monday, 47 miles on Tuesday, 56 miles on Wednesday, 39 miles on Thursday, and 61 miles on Friday. About how many miles did she drive altogether that week?

2. (*to the hundreds' place*) At Trent High School, there are 824 students from Latin America, 367 students from Asia, 89 students from Europe, and 1390 students from the United States. Estimate:

    a. how many students are from Latin America
    b. how many students are from Asia
    c. how many students are from United States
    d. the total student population

3. (*to the ten thousands' place*) Riley's salary for the first year was $26,529, for the second year it was $28,986, for the third year it was $34,112, and for the fourth year it was $39,821. Approximate his salary for:

    a. the first year
    b. the second year
    c. the third year
    d. the fourth year
    e. all four years

4. (*to the thousands' place*) Kimberly bought a car last year for $16,927. She sold it this year for $12,291. Estimate what she:
   a. paid for the car last year
   b. sold the car for this year

Exercise 3-G   STUDENTS, STUDENTS, STUDENTS . . .

There are three high schools in Greenville: Poly High, Tech High, and Hoover High.

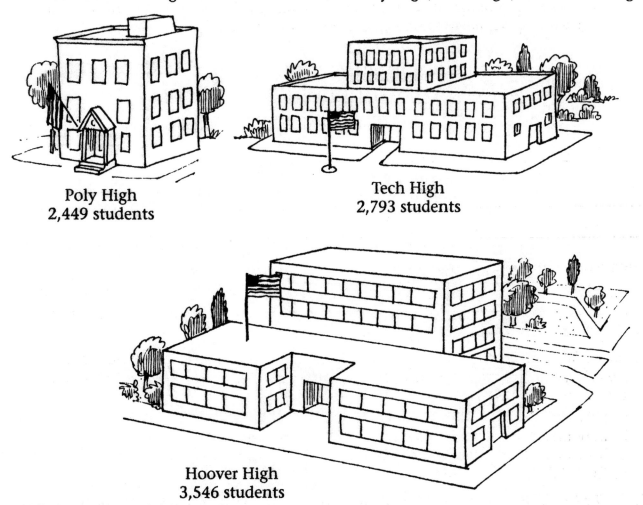

Poly High
2,449 students

Tech High
2,793 students

Hoover High
3,546 students

1. How many students attend Tech High?
2. What is the population of Hoover High?
3. What is the population of Poly High and Hoover High together?
4. What is the population of all three high schools together?
5. Round answer 1 to the nearest hundreds' place.
6. Round answer 2 to the nearest hundreds' place.
7. Round answer 3 to the nearest thousands' place.

8. Round answer 4 to the nearest ten thousands' place.

9. Which school has the greatest number of students?

10. Which school has the least number of students?

LISTEN!

Your teacher will ask you questions. Listen. Then on your own paper, write the letter that appears next to the correct answer.

1. a. infinite
   b. billion
   c. million

2. a. exact
   b. equal
   c. about

3. a. numbers
   b. zeros
   c. digits

4. a. two
   b. three
   c. four

5. a. greatest
   b. least
   c. equal

6. a. ones
   b. tens
   c. hundreds

7. a. smallest
   b. greatest
   c. infinite

8. a. zero
   b. end
   c. infinite

9. a. equal
   b. ordinal number
   c. lower

10. a. how big
    b. what kind
    c. what order

LET'S TALK ABOUT ...

1. number line

2. infinite

3. round off

4. estimate

5. approximate

6. nearest

7. round number

8. greater than

9. less than

10. underline

Round off to the nearest tens' place.

1. 54
2. 25
3. 61
4. 19
5. 241
6. 375
7. 950
8. 216
9. 1,582
10. 649
11. 906
12. 95

Round off to the nearest hundreds' place.

13. 425
14. 850
15. 668
16. 2,711
17. 1,074
18. 5,802
19. 975
20. 55,251

Round off to the nearest thousands' place.

21. 6,421
22. 2,911
23. 8,909
24. 5,500
25. 14,327
26. 26,821
27. 352,911
28. 20,450
29. 75,700
30. 729,700

Unit 1 Vocabulary Words

1. Approximate   An estimate.

2. Cardinal Number   A number (one, two, three, . . .) used for counting and answers the question, "How many?"

3. Couple   Two (people or things).

4. Digit   Any of the numbers 0, 1, 2, 3, 4, 5, 6, 7, 8, 9.

5. Double   Two together.

6. Dozen   Twelve of something.

7. Estimate   Approximation.

8. Half-Dozen   Six of something.

9. Ordinal Number   A number which tells order (1st, 2nd, 3rd, . . .).

10. Pair   Two things of a kind (socks, people, animals, . . .).

11. Place Name   In the number 345, the *place name* of 3 is hundreds.

12. Place Value   In the number 345, the *place value* of 3 is 300.

13. Quadruplets   A group of four of the same thing or kind.

14. Round Number   A number ending in one or more zeros, as 40, 350, or 5,000.

15. Single   One of something or a person who is not married.

16. Triple   Three together.

17. Triplets   A group of three of the same thing or kind.

18. Twins   A group of two of the same thing or kind.

<u>Operations with Whole Numbers</u>

1 2 3 4 5 6 7 8 9 0 π

1234567890⌐

1234567890∡

1234567890+

1234567890√

0123456789÷

√0987654321

+0987654321

∡0987654321

⌐0987654321

π0987654321

4   Addition

4-1   Language of Addition

This is an **addition** problem:

$$6 + 2 = 8$$

We say: "Six plus two equals eight."

The *sum* is 8. The *addends* are 6 and 2.

What is the *sum* of 3 and 4?

The sum of 3 and 4 is 7.

Exercise 4-A

Complete each sentence.

1. The ___sum___ of nine and four is thirteen.
2. Five _____ six equals eleven.
3. Seven plus three _____ ten.
4. The sum of three and eight is _____.
5. Ten _____ ten _____ twenty.
6. The sum of _____ and six is ten.
7. Three _____ four _____ seven.
8. The _____ of thirteen and three _____ sixteen.
9. Nine _____ six _____ fifteen.
10. _____ plus eight _____ twenty-eight.

Answer each question.

11. What is the sum of six and five?   *eleven*
12. What is the sum of fourteen and nine?
13. What is the sum of eleven and eight?
14. What is the sum of seven and seven?

15. What is the sum of fifteen and three?

16. What is the sum of four and sixteen?

17. What is the sum of nine and zero?

18. What is the sum of seven and eight?

19. What is the sum of sixteen and six?

20. What is the sum of twelve and twelve?

Write with *words.*

21. $2 + 3 = 5$ *Two plus three equals five* or
    The sum of two and three is five.

22. $7 + 5 = 12$

23. $0 + 10 = 10$

24. $13 + 8 = 21$

25. $17 + 9 = 26$

26. $24 + 6 = 30$

27. $55 + 6 = 61$

28. $18 + 9 = 27$

29. $42 + 3 = 45$

30. $94 + 10 = 104$

Complete.

31. $13 + 2 = 15$ Addends: ___ and ___   Sum: ___

32. $12 + 5 = 17$ Addends: ___ and ___   Sum: ___

33. $0 + 11 = 11$ Addends: ___ and ___   Sum: ___

34. $16 + 4 = 20$ Addends: ___ and ___   Sum: ___

4-2 Commutative Property of Addition

Look at the following:

$$5 + 6 = 11 \qquad 6 + 5 = 11$$
If we add $5 + 6$, the sum is 11.
If we add $6 + 5$, the sum is 11.

$$5 + 6 = 6 + 5$$
The sums are equal.

The *order* of adding numbers does not change the sum.

COMMUTATIVE PROPERTY OF ADDITION:

We can add numbers in any order. For all numbers a and b:

$$a + b = b + a$$

DEFINITION: Parentheses

Parentheses ( ), group numbers together. We add together the numbers that are inside the parentheses:

$$(2 + 3) + 6 =$$
$$5 + 6 = 11$$

Exercise 4-B

Add the numbers inside the parentheses and find the sum:

1. $(3 + 4) + 6 = \underline{7} + \underline{6} = \underline{13}$
2. $6 + (4 + 7) = \underline{} + \underline{} = \underline{}$
3. $2 + (9 + 8) = \underline{} + \underline{} = \underline{}$
4. $(1 + 7) + 3 = \underline{} + \underline{} = \underline{}$
5. $3 + (4 + 8) + 2 = \underline{} + \underline{} + \underline{} = \underline{}$
6. $(4 + 5) + (3 + 7) = \underline{} + \underline{} = \underline{}$
7. $(2 + 6) + 9 + (8 + 1) = \underline{} + \underline{} + \underline{} = \underline{}$
8. $6 + (1 + 5 + 3) + 4 = \underline{} + \underline{} + \underline{} = \underline{}$

4-3 | Associative Property of Addition

We can group $2 + 3 + 1$ in these ways:

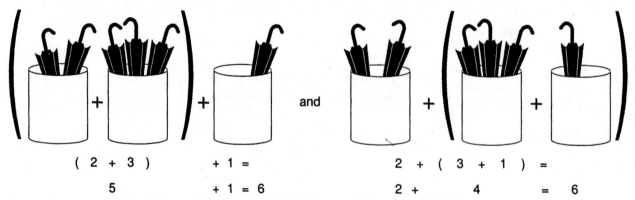

(2 + 3)   + 1 =   and   2 + (3 + 1) =

5   + 1 = 6   2 +   4   = 6

The sums are equal.

ASSOCIATIVE PROPERTY OF ADDITION:

If we group three or more numbers in different ways and add them together, the sum does not change. For all numbers a, b, and c:

$$(a + b) + c = a + (b + c)$$

40

$$3 + 0 = 3$$
$$0 + 5 = 5$$
$$6 = 6 + 0$$

ADDITIVE IDENTITY PROPERTY OF ADDITION:

Adding zero to any number does not change the value of the number. For all numbers a:

$$a + 0 = a$$

Exercise 4-C

Fill in the numbers, then write the property shown: commutative, associative, or additive identity.

1. $7 + \underline{6} = 6 + 7$ $\underline{Commutative}$

2. $(4 + 3) + 6 = 4 + (\underline{\ \ } + 6)$ _____

3. $0 + 4 = \underline{\ \ }$ _____

4. $7 + (9 + 3) = (7 + \underline{\ \ }) + 3$ _____

5. $(6 + 4) + 5 = 5 + (\underline{\ \ } + 4)$ _____

6. $19 + \underline{\ \ } = 19$ _____

7. $17 + 11 = \underline{\ \ } + 17$ _____

8. $(x + 6) + y = x + (6 + \underline{\ \ })$ _____

9. $39 + 14 = \underline{\ \ } + 39$ _____

10. $(r + s) + t = t + (\underline{\ \ } + r)$ _____

11. $11 + 0 = \underline{\ \ }$ _____

12. $6 + (9 + 4) = (9 + \underline{\ \ }) + 6$ _____

13. $(2 + x) + p = \underline{\ \ } + (2 + x)$ _____

14. $0 + 8 = 8 + \underline{\ \ }$ _____

15. $p + m + (r + q) = p + (m + \underline{\ \ }) + q$ _____

16. $10 + 6 + 7 = 7 + 6 + \underline{\ \ }$ _____

17. $\underline{\ \ } + 21 = 21$ _____

18. $(a + c + d) + e = e + (a + \underline{\ \ } + d)$ _____

LET'S TALK ABOUT ...

1. addition
2. plus
3. addends
4. sum

5. commutative
6. associative
7. additive identity
8. parentheses

Exercise 4-D

Add the following numbers:

1. 7 + 3 + 2
2. 9 + 6 + 4
3. 1 + 6 + 3
4. 2 + 8 + 7
5. 6 + 5 + 2
6. 4 + 3 + 2 + 5
7. 3 + 6 + 7 + 2
8. 1 + 9 + 5 + 4

9. 6 + 3 + 7 + 2
10. 8 + 5 + 2 + 6
11. 4 + 7 + 8 + 9
12. 8 + 2 + 7 + 2
13. 3 + 6 + 6 + 3
14. 9 + 2 + 1 + 5
15. 2 + 7 + 8 + 4
16. 6 + 7 + 8 + 5

17.
```
   23
 + 15
```

18.
```
   45
 + 23
```

19.
```
   16
 + 31
```

20.
```
   32
 + 67
```

21.
```
   16
 +  3
```

22.
```
   87
 + 12
```

23.
```
   21
 + 43
```

24.
```
   46
 + 32
```

25.
```
   73
 + 15
```

26.
```
   82
 + 23
```

27.
```
  233
 + 142
```

28.
```
  426
 + 132
```

29.
```
  127
 + 542
```

30.
```
  567
 + 121
```

31.
```
  342
 + 211
```

32.
```
  361
 + 215
```

33.
```
  123
  210
 + 734
```

34.
```
  303
  124
 + 432
```

35.
```
  625
  231
 + 113
```

36.
```
  326
  431
 + 131
```

37.
```
  110
  454
 + 135
```

38.
```
  306
  210
 + 153
```

39.
```
  524
  231
 + 242
```

40.
```
  364
  122
 + 410
```

41.
```
  531
  120
 + 243
```

42.	422	45.	1,233	48.	12,423
	511		2,412		2,422
	+ 222		+ 3,211		+ 1,131
43.	743	46.	2,534	49.	30,133
	102		1,233		2,425
	+ 133		+ 5,122		+ 1,211
44.	320	47.	22,655	50.	23,334
	335		24,211		+ 1,422
	+ 214		+ 13,122		

4-5 | Addition With Carrying

Example:

```
    4 3
  + 2 9
```

Add the numbers in the ones' place: 3 + 9 = 12.
Write the 2 in the ones' place and *carry* the 1 to the
   tens' place:

```
    1
    4 3
  + 2 9
      2
```

Add the numbers in the tens' place: 1 + 4 + 2 = 7.
Write the 7 in the tens' place:

```
    1
    4 3
  + 2 9
    7 2
```

Example:

```
    3 4 5
  + 7 9 8
```

Add the numbers in the ones' place: 5 + 8 = 13.
Write the 3 in the ones' place and *carry* the 1 to the
   tens' place:

```
      1
    3 4 5
  + 7 9 8
        3
```

Add the numbers in the tens' place: 1 + 4 + 9 = 14.
Write the 4 in the tens' place and *carry* the 1 to the
   hundreds' place:

```
    1 1
    3 4 5
  + 7 9 8
      4 3
```

Add the numbers in the hundreds' place: 1 + 3 + 7 = 11.
   Write the digits in the hundreds' and
   thousands' places:

```
    1 1
    3 4 5
  + 7 9 8
  1 , 1 4 3
```

Exercise 4-E

Add the following numbers:

1.	54 + 95	8.	18 + 36	15.	349 +388
2.	67 + 45	9.	34 + 78	16.	277 +366
3.	99 + 99	10.	75 + 75	17.	590 +888
4.	27 + 59	11.	27 + 66	18.	357 +927
5.	38 + 92	12.	456 +568	19.	544 +878
6.	89 + 98	13.	678 +877	20.	909 +909
7.	27 + 66	14.	943 +795	21.	238 +455

22.	366 +128	28.	767 388 +955
23.	543 122 +822	29.	4,768 1,499 + 4,576
24.	465 134 +989	30.	5,722 1,877 + 7,633
25.	672 195 +458	31.	7,251 4,900 + 8,123
26.	930 155 +988	32.	1,659 4,612 + 7,498
27.	432 176 +903		

Exercise 4-F

Add the following numbers:

1. 64 + 159 + 307 + 14
2. 195 + 36 + 2,496
3. 849 + 1,566 + 82
4. 1,927 + 349 + 211
5. 607 + 94 + 8,422
6. 7,431 + 3,206 + 11 + 419
7. 644 + 72 + 1,899
8. 14 + 267 + 396
9. 611 + 924 + 3,264
10. 98 + 88 + 329 + 11
11. 521 + 2,314 + 101
12. 7,327 + 2,433 + 95
13. 693 + 4,207 + 143
14. 27 + 869 + 39 + 492
15. 9,366 + 321 + 4,070
16. 10,322 + 8,011 + 694
17. 175 + 13,012 + 96
18. 429 + 7,863 + 345
19. 16,500 + 399 + 4,631
20. 7,053 + 29 + 398
21. 587 + 3,779 + 348
22. 19,011 + 5,468 + 13
23. 6,344 + 19,993 + 27
24. 782 + 9,399 + 4,711

Example:

Yesterday, Norma worked 8 hours. Today she worked 10 hours. How many hours did she work **altogether**?

The word *altogether* tells us that this is an addition problem. We add the hours together:

$$
\begin{array}{r}
2\ 6 \\
+\ \ 1\ 8 \\
\hline
\end{array}
$$

Answer: 4 4 hours

Example:

Sergio's basketball team scored 34 points in Game 1. In Game 2, they scored 62 points, and in Game 3, they scored 54 points. What were the **total** *points scored for all three games?*

The word *total* tells us that this is an addition problem. Add:

$$
\begin{array}{r}
3\ 4 \\
6\ 2 \\
+\ \ 5\ 4 \\
\hline
\end{array}
$$

Answer: 1 5 0 points

Example:

Mayra needs school supplies! The books cost $35, the pencils cost $4, the pens cost $11, and the paper costs $15. What is the **combined** *cost of all the school supplies?*

The word *combined* tells us to add:

$$
\begin{array}{r}
\$\ 3\ 5 \\
4 \\
1\ 1 \\
+\ \ 1\ 5 \\
\hline
\end{array}
$$

Answer: $ 6 5

Raymond Lopez is an eleventh-grade student at North Hills HIgh School. There are students from Latin America, Europe, Asia, and the United States in his math class. Solve each problem below and show all of your work.

Raymond's math class

From:	Latin America	Asia	Europe	United States	
Number of girls	8	3	2	5	18
Number of boys	6	5	1	7	+19

1. Altogether, how many girls are there in the class?

2. How many boys are there from Asia, Europe, and the United States?

3. Are there more students (boys and girls) from the United States or from Latin America?

4. How many students are there in the class altogether?

5. What is the total number of boys in the class?

6. Are there more boys or girls in the class?

In November, Raymond took four math tests. Look at his test scores.

	Test 1	Test 2	Test 3	Test 4
Raymond's scores	37	32	30	38
Total possible	40	40	40	40

7. What is the total possible score for the first three tests combined?

8. What is Raymond's combined test scores for the first three tests?

9. Did Raymond do better on test 2 or on test 3?

10. Which test shows Raymond's highest score?

11. Which test shows Raymond's lowest score?

North Hills High School is a four-year high school. The student population is:

	9th grade	10th grade	11th grade	12th grade
Number of girls	340	336	249	235
Number of boys	377	322	325	268

12. How many boys and girls are there in the:
    a. ninth grade?
    b. tenth grade?
    c. eleventh grade?
    d. twelfth grade?

13. How many boys are there altogether in grades 9 through 12 (9, 10, 11, 12)?

14. How many girls are there altogether in grades 9 through 12 (9, 10, 11, 12)?

15. What is the total school population?

16. Which grade level has the:
    a. greatest number of students?
    b. least number of students?

| Exercise 4-H   Problem Solving with Addition: CLASS TRIP! |

The seniors at North Hills High School take a class trip to Blackburn each year. North Hills High is located in Redmond City. Look at the map below and answer the questions.

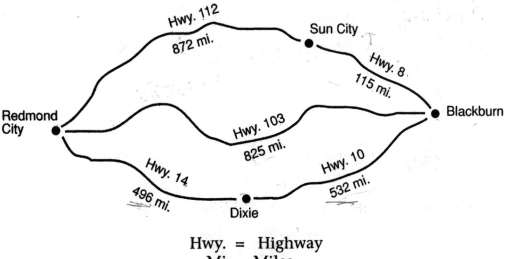

Hwy. = Highway
Mi. = Miles

1. There are three ways to travel from Redmond to Blackburn:
   Highway ___ and Highway ___
   Highway ___
   Highway ___ and Highway ___

2. How many miles do the students travel if they take:
   a. Highway 112 and Highway 8?
   b. Highway 103?
   c. Highway 14 and Highway 10?

3. Which way has the *least* number of miles?

4. Which way has the *most* number of miles?

5. Some of the students will travel from Redmond City to Sun City, and then to Blackburn. From Blackburn, they will go to Dixie. How many miles will they travel altogether?

6. How many miles is a round trip from Redmond City to Blackburn (on Highway 112 and Highway 8), then back to Redmond City?

7. How many miles is a round trip from Redmond City to Blackburn (on Highway 112 and Highway 8), then back to Redmond City (on Highway 10 and Highway 14)?

47

1. Raymond's Math Club has 27 girls. There are 13 more boys than girls in the club.
   a. How many boys are there in the Math Club?
   b. How many students are there altogether in the Math Club?

2. The Math Club has $67 to spend. Math books cost $13, math games cost $18, computer paper costs $24, and a calculator costs $23.
   a. Do they have enough money to buy the computer paper, calculator, and math games?
   b. How much will the math books, math games, computer paper, and calculator cost altogether?
   c. Do they have enough money to buy everything?
   d. The students spent $55. What items did they buy?

3. Each week, the students play math games with their computer. There are six teams of students. Look at the following point totals for each team.

	Team 1	Team 2	Team 3	Team 4	Team 5	Team 6
Week 1	13,246	12,499	5,294	10,324	8,020	10,244
Week 2	11,597	13,006	13,107	9,261	14,768	11,724
Week 3	12,698	5,772	13,624	14,920	6,492	12,324
Week 4	7,339	11,977	9,021	6,792	12,931	6,549

   a. How many points did Team 2 score altogether in weeks 1, 2, 3, and 4?
   b. Look at week 2. Which team scored the most points?
   c. How many points did Team 4 score for the first two weeks?
   d. Which team scored more points altogether: Team 4 or Team 5?
   e. Which team scored more points in weeks 2 and 3 combined: Team 1 or Team 4?
   f. Look at the scores for Team 1. Round each score to the nearest *hundreds'* place:

   Week 1 _____   Week 3 _____

   Week 2 _____   Week 4 _____

   g. Look at week 4. Add the scores for each team and round the total to the nearest *ten thousands'* place.
   h. Add the total score for Team 6 and round to the nearest *thousands'* place.

48

Write with words.

1. 7 + 3 = 10

2. 13 + 7 = 20

3. 14 + 8 = 22

4. 12 + 13 = 25

5. 11 + 23 = 34

6. 19 + 22 = 41

Complete.

7. 15 + 6 = 21   Addends: ___ and ___   Sum: ___

Add.

8. 13 + 4

9. 25 + 9

10. 46 + 12

11. 57 + 11

12. 96 + 47

13. 435 + 283

14. 295 + 234 + 34

15. 803 + 67 + 21

16. 1,256 + 382

17. 7,355 + 466 + 89

18. 8,534 + 3,455

19. 24,544 + 5,643

20. 34,551 + 3,500

21. 867,773 + 243,775

22. 35,488 + 2,344 + 144

Write which property is shown: commutative, associative, or additive identity

23. $4 + 3 = 3 + 4$

24. $0 + 19 = 19$

25. $8 + (3 + 2) = (8 + 3) + 2$

26. $x = 0 + x$

27. $m + (r + q) = (m + r) + q$

28. $(s + t + x) + w = w + (s + t + x)$

29. Erica works in a bookstore. She sells books and magazines. Here are her sales for 1 week:

	Monday	Tuesday	Wednesday	Thursday	Friday
Books:	29	16	33	14	68
Magazines:	23	45	17	33	58

a. How many books did she sell in the first three days? (Monday, Tuesday, and Wednesday)

b. Which day did Erica sell the *greatest* number of books?

c. Which day did Erica sell the *least* number of books?

d. How many magazines did she sell *in all?*

e. Did she sell more books or magazines on Tuesday?

f. How many books did she sell *in all?*

g. What is the total number of books and magazines that Erica sold for that week?

5 Subtraction

5-1 Language of Subtraction

This is a **subtraction** problem:

$$7 - 2 = 5$$

We say: "Seven minus two equals five."
The *difference* is 5. The *minuend* is 7. The *subtrahend* is 2.

What is the *difference* of 8 and 5?

The difference of 8 and 5 is 3.

Exercise 5-A

Complete each sentence.

1. The __difference__ of nine and three is six.
2. Six _____ four equals two.
3. Ten minus five _____ five.
4. The difference of eleven and seven is _____.
5. Fifteen _____ five _____ ten.
6. The _____ of twelve and six _____ six.
7. Eighteen _____ nine _____ nine.
8. _____ minus six equals two.
9. The difference of thirteen and six is _____.
10. Twenty-four _____ twenty _____ four.

Answer each question.

11. What is the difference of eight and two?   *six*
12. What is the difference of seven and six?
13. What is the difference of nineteen and ten?
14. What is the difference of fifteen and nine?

15. What is the difference of eleven and eleven?

16. What is the difference of eighteen and zero?

17. What is the difference of thirty-one and five?

18. What is the difference of sixty-four and twenty?

19. What is the difference of thirty-three and eight?

20. What is the difference of ninety and eighty?

Write with *words*.

21. $7 - 4 = 3$ *Seven minus four equals three,* or
                    The difference of seven and four is three.

22. $15 - 5 = 10$

23. $11 - 3 = 8$

24. $27 - 4 = 23$

25. $47 - 7 = 40$

26. $15 - 15 = 0$

27. $95 - 10 = 85$

28. $73 - 6 = 67$

29. $52 - 12 = 40$

30. $12 - 0 = 12$

Complete.

31. $12 - 8 = 4$ Minuend: ___   Subtrahend: ___   Difference: ___

32. $18 - 3 = 15$ Minuend: ___   Subtrahend: ___   Difference: ___

33. $19 - 9 = 10$ Minuend: ___   Subtrahend: ___   Difference: ___

34. $13 - 0 = 13$ Minuend: ___   Subtrahend: ___   Difference: ___

5-2 Subtraction of Whole Numbers

Example:
$$\begin{array}{r} 7\ 4 \\ -\ 3\ 2 \\ \hline \end{array}$$

Subtract the numbers in the ones' place: $4 - 2 = 2$.
Write the 2 in the ones' place:
$$\begin{array}{r} 7\ 4 \\ -\ 3\ 2 \\ \hline 2 \end{array}$$

Subtract the numbers in the tens' place: $7 - 3 = 4$.
Write the 4 in the tens' place:
$$\begin{array}{r} 7\ 4 \\ -\ 3\ 2 \\ \hline 4\ 2 \end{array}$$

To check your answer, add the difference (42) to the subtrahend (32). The sum should equal the minuend (74).

$$
\begin{array}{r}
7\ 4 \\
-\ \ 3\ 2 \\
\hline
4\ 2 \\
+\ \ 3\ 2 \\
\hline
7\ 4
\end{array}
$$

Exercise 5-B

Subtract the following numbers. Check your answers by adding.

1. 13 – 7
2. 11 – 4
3. 18 – 6
4. 14 – 7
5. 12 – 6
6. 11 – 7
7. 15 – 8
8. 18 – 9

9. 12 – 4
10. 11 – 9
11. 10 – 6
12. 15 – 6
13. 13 – 8
14. 16 – 9
15. 17 – 8
16. 15 – 7

17.	13 – 2	23.	75 – 24	29.	467 – 302	35.	459 – 354	41.	977 – 153
18.	34 – 3	24.	87 – 64	30.	948 – 732	36.	966 – 833	42.	757 – 245
19.	95 – 4	25.	36 – 21	31.	549 – 338	37.	784 – 320	43.	820 – 310
20.	85 – 3	26.	54 – 44	32.	677 – 321	38.	741 – 620	44.	563 – 111
21.	98 – 2	27.	465 – 322	33.	784 – 643	39.	688 – 521	45.	888 – 666
22.	56 – 22	28.	957 – 244	34.	653 – 253	40.	762 – 632	46.	743 – 312

Example:
```
   4 3
 - 1 8
```

Look at the numbers in the ones' place. We cannot subtract 8 from 3. We must *borrow* from the tens' place. The 4 in the tens' place tells us that there are 4 tens. We *borrow* 1 ten, or 10, leaving 3 in the tens' place:

```
  3
  4 3
- 1 8
```

We add 10 + 3 (10 that we borrowed plus 3 in the ones' place). 10 + 3 = 13.

```
 3 13
  4 3
- 1 8
```

Now we can subtract. 13 – 8 = 5. Write the 5 in the ones' place. 3 – 1 = 2. Write the 2 in the tens' place. The answer is 25:

```
 3 13
  4 3
- 1 8
  2 5
```

Check your answer:

```
   4 3
 - 1 8
   2 5
 + 1 8
   4 3
```

Example:
```
   3 2 6
 - 1 6 8
```

Look at the numbers in the ones' place. We cannot subtract 8 from 6. We must *borrow* 1 ten, or 10, from the tens' place, leaving 1 ten. We add the 10 to 6 in the ones' place. (10 + 6 = 16), and subtract 8 from 16. (16 – 8 = 8)

```
    1 16
  3 2 6
- 1 6 8
      8
```

Look at the numbers in the tens' place. We cannot subtract 6 tens from 1 ten. We must *borrow* 1 hundred (or 10 tens) from the hundreds' place, leaving 2 hundreds. We add 10 + 1 (10 that we borrowed plus 1 in the tens' place). 10 + 1 = 11.

```
  2 11 16
  3 2 6
- 1 6 8
      8
```

Subtract 6 from 11. Write the 5 in the tens' place. 2 – 1 = 1. Write the 1 in the hundreds' place. The answer is 158:

```
  2 11 16
  3 2 6
- 1 6 8
  1 5 8
```

Check your answer:

```
    3 2 6
 -  1 6 8
    1 5 8
 +  1 6 8
    3 2 6
```

Subtract the numbers. Check your answers by adding.

1.	54 − 8	8.	71 − 59	15.	534 − 329	22.	523 − 376
2.	73 − 7	9.	35 − 16	16.	922 − 688	23.	471 − 188
3.	62 − 9	10.	82 − 36	17.	617 − 499	24.	233 − 127
4.	91 − 77	11.	96 − 79	18.	411 − 377	25.	412 − 289
5.	53 − 8	12.	54 − 39	19.	525 − 489	26.	311 − 278
6.	83 − 49	13.	544 − 288	20.	541 − 337	27.	535 − 417
7.	94 − 78	14.	621 − 307	21.	921 − 699		

Subtract the numbers. Check by adding.

28. 345 − 67
29. 287 − 109
30. 714 − 575

31. 342 − 77
32. 511 − 78
33. 476 − 183

34. 245 − 67
35. 123 − 56
36. 2,541 − 866

Subtract the numbers. Check by adding.

1.   433
   – 264
	7. 6,433
	   – 2,799
		13. 67,122
		   – 34,784
			19. 864,218
			   – 438,628

2.   321
   – 199
	8. 8,111
	   – 7,277
		14. 37,811
		   – 28,733
			20. 499,321
			   – 89,555

3.   743
   – 298
	9. 23,451
	   – 19,376
		15. 125,677
		   – 45,877
			21. 354,958
			   – 244,976

4.   6,822
   – 2,767
	10. 75,624
	   – 56,766
		16. 961,833
		   – 171,566
			22. 47,283
			   – 6,512

5.   3,512
   – 1,287
	11. 32,471
	   – 20,488
		17. 129,863
		   – 49,127
			23. 5,421,773
			   – 983,887

6.   4,343
   – 1,879
	12. 45,381
	   – 13,866
		18. 457,218
		   – 70,651
			24. 4,338,219
			   – 4,176,989

Subtract the numbers. Check by adding.

25. 3,122 – 373
26. 45,677 – 2,338
27. 12,339 – 2,778

28. 3,544 – 1,879
29. 456,921 – 3,876
30. 12,512 – 9,455

31. 17,433 – 9,877
32. 143,566,112 – 45,677
33. 1,243,123 – 997,987

5-4 Subtraction with Borrowing from Zeros

Example:

$$\begin{array}{r} 3\ 0\ 2 \\ -\ 1\ 8\ 5 \end{array}$$

Look at the numbers in the ones' place. We cannot subtract 5 from 2. We cannot borrow from the tens' place (0), so we must borrow 1 hundred from the hundreds' place (10 tens) first and add it to the tens' place.

$$\begin{array}{r} {}^{2}\ {}^{10} \\ \cancel{3}\ \cancel{0}\ 2 \\ -\ 1\ 8\ 5 \end{array}$$

Now we can borrow 1 ten (10 ones) from the tens' place, leaving 9 tens. We add 10 + 2 (10 that we borrowed plus 2 in the ones' place). 10 + 2 = 12.

$$\begin{array}{r} {}^{9} \\ {}^{2}\ \cancel{10}\ {}^{12} \\ \cancel{3}\ \cancel{0}\ \cancel{2} \\ -\ 1\ 8\ 5 \end{array}$$

Subtract 5 from 12 in the ones' place. (12 − 5 = 7).
Subtract 8 from 9 in the tens' place. (9 − 8 = 1).
Subtract 1 from 2 in the hundreds' place. (2 − 1 = 1).
The answer is 117.

```
        9
    2  ᴎ 12
    3  9  2
  −  1  8  5
     1  1  7
```

Check your answer:

```
      3  0  2
  −   1  8  5
      1  1  7
  +   1  8  5
      3  0  2
```

Example: 6 , 0 0 0
          −   3 5 8

We cannot subtract 8 from 0 in the ones' place. We cannot borrow from the tens' or hundreds' places. We must borrow 1 thousand (10 hundreds) from the thousands' place and add it to the hundreds' place.

```
   5     10
   6 ,   0  0  0
  −      3  5  8
```

Now we borrow 1 hundred (10 tens) from the hundreds' place, leaving 9 hundreds, and add it to the tens' place.

```
           9
   5      ᴎ  10
   6 ,   0  0  0
  −      3  5  8
```

Then we borrow 1 ten (10 ones) from the tens' place, leaving 9 tens, and add it to the ones' place. Subtract the numbers and the answer is 5642.

```
           9  9
   5      ᴎ  ᴎ  10
   6 ,   0  0  0
  −      3  5  8
   5 ,   6  4  2
```

Check your answer:

```
   6 , 0  0  0
  −     3  5  8
   5 , 6  4  2
  +     3  5  8
   6 , 0  0  0
```

Subtract and check your answers by adding.

1.	40 – 19	10.	301 – 187	19.	8,000 – 2,799
2.	30 – 13	11.	502 – 284	20.	2,006 – 1,888
3.	700 – 212	12.	700 – 484	21.	3,070 – 1,664
4.	90 – 48	13.	4,704 – 2,439	22.	51,007 – 7,668
5.	906 – 537	14.	5,000 – 2,896	23.	27,103 – 17,195
6.	600 – 156	15.	4,002 – 3,827	24.	623,400 – 551,982
7.	505 – 499	16.	2,000 – 1,987	25.	700,000 – 643,797
8.	800 – 356	17.	6,001 – 5,992	26.	450,702 – 387,288
9.	200 – 138	18.	5,020 – 3,887	27.	400,400 – 274,661

Subtract.

28. 400 – 287   31. 4,000 – 3,892   34. 700,090 – 3,716

29. 5,400 – 2,367   32. 5,090 – 765   35. 30,000 – 4,728

30. 340,800 – 2,367   33. 1,900,000 – 8,211   36. 5,300,000 – 654,677

5-5 Inverse Operations

Addition and subtraction are **inverse operations**. Each subtraction problem has its *inverse addition* problem.

Subtraction	*Inverse Operation (Addition)*
5 – 3 = 2	2 + 3 = 5
12 – 9 = 3	3 + 9 = 12

In Exercises 5-B through 5-E, we used the *inverse operation* of subtraction to check our answers.

Example:

$$\begin{array}{r} 12 \\ -8 \\ \hline 4 \end{array}$$

Check by inverse operation:

$$\begin{array}{r} 8 \\ +4 \\ \hline 12 \end{array}$$

Exercise 5-F

Check each problem by writing an *inverse* addition problem

1. $6 - 5 = 1$ *$1 + 5 = 6$*
2. $8 - 3 = 5$
3. $11 - 6 = 5$
4. $12 - 6 = 6$
5. $8 - 0 = 8$
6. $24 - 18 = 6$
7. $13 - 13 = 0$
8. $23 - 1 = 22$
9. $14 - 8 = 6$
10. $16 - 10 = 6$

5-6 Using Inverse Operations to Find Missing Numbers

We can use *inverse operations* to find missing numbers.

Example: $\_\_ - 4 = 7$

Use the inverse operation:

$$7 + 4 = 11$$

Answer: $\underline{11} - 4 = 7$

Exercise 5-G

Use the inverse operation to find the missing numbers.

1. $\_\_ - 4 = 13$
2. $\_\_ - 6 = 22$
3. $\_\_ - 9 = 29$
4. $\_\_ - 5 = 33$
5. $\_\_ - 13 = 44$
6. $\_\_ - 10 = 57$
7. $\_\_ - 26 = 68$
8. $\_\_ - 35 = 198$
9. $\_\_ - 22 = 104$
10. $\_\_ - 54 = 94$
11. $\_\_ - 67 = 345$
12. $\_\_ - 76 = 399$
13. $\_\_ - 25 = 450$
14. $\_\_ - 0 = 399$
15. $\_\_ - 122 = 768$
16. $\_\_ - 521 = 673$
17. $\_\_ - 744 = 0$
18. $\_\_ - 291 = 291$

Example:

*Use the **inverse operation** to find the missing number.*

$$12 + \underline{} = 15$$

Use the inverse operation:

$$15 - 12 = 3$$

Answer: $12 + \underline{3} = 15$

Exercise 5-H

Use the inverse operation to find the missing numbers.

1. $5 + \underline{} = 14$
2. $11 + \underline{} = 34$
3. $9 + \underline{} = 22$
4. $13 + \underline{} = 36$
5. $24 + \underline{} = 44$
6. $\underline{} + 12 = 55$

7. $\underline{} + 67 = 87$
8. $45 + \underline{} = 45$
9. $\underline{} + 66 = 156$
10. $\underline{} + 35 = 129$
11. $89 + \underline{} = 213$
12. $76 + \underline{} = 166$

13. $\underline{} + 188 = 412$
14. $\underline{} + 106 = 339$
15. $88 + \underline{} = 631$
16. $377 + \underline{} = 599$
17. $\underline{} + 433 = 967$
18. $562 + \underline{} = 1,584$

Exercise 5-I

Find the missing number using inverse operation.

1. $34 + \underline{} = 48$
2. $\underline{} - 15 = 39$
3. $\underline{} + 56 = 78$
4. $67 + \underline{} = 125$
5. $\underline{} - 56 = 27$
6. $78 + \underline{} = 78$
7. $\underline{} - 124 = 0$
8. $\underline{} + 92 = 381$

9. $\underline{} - 67 = 53$
10. $377 + \underline{} = 935$
11. $\underline{} + 271 = 271$
12. $\underline{} - 655 = 1,298$
13. $\underline{} + 874 = 2,366$
14. $\underline{} - 377 = 872$
15. $982 + \underline{} = 5,499$
16. $873 + \underline{} = 984$

17. $\underline{} - 659 = 0$
18. $\underline{} - 3,455 = 365$
19. $721 + \underline{} = 1,344$
20. $988 + \underline{} = 988$
21. $\underline{} - 734 = 21$
22. $\underline{} + 1,569 = 4,578$
23. $\underline{} - 312 = 312$
24. $\underline{} - 937 = 0$

Complete the sentences with the following words:

minuend	subtrahend	addends
plus	inverse	sum
associative	commutative	subtraction
addition	minus	additive identity

1. The _____ is the answer in an addition problem.

2. We read "+" as _____.

3. 6 + 2 = 2 + 6 is an example of the _____ property.

4. In a _____ problem, the answer is called the difference.

5. Twelve _____ ten equals two.

6. The numbers that we add together are called _____.

7. The numbers that we subtract are called the _____ and the _____.

8. (7 + 3) + 1 = 7 + (3 + 1) is an example of the _____ property.

9. 6 + 3 = 9 is an example of an _____ problem.

10. The _____ operation of 5 − 3 = 2 is 3 + 2 = 5.

11. 7 + 0 = 7 is an example of the _____ property.

LET'S TALK ABOUT ...

1. subtraction

2. minus

3. difference

4. minuend

5. subtrahend

6. inverse operation

7. borrow

8. carry

Example:

*Jason got 23 correct on Thursday's spelling test. He got 32 correct on Friday's spelling test. **How many more** words did he get correct on Friday?*

The words *how many more* tells us that this is a subtraction problem. We subtract the scores:

$$\begin{array}{r} 3\ 2 \\ -\ 2\ 3 \\ \hline \end{array}$$

Answer: 9 more words correct

Example:

*Mr. Tonak drove 1,245 miles last year. He drove 1,987 miles this year. What is the **difference** in mileage for both years?*

The word *difference* tells us to subtract:

$$\begin{array}{r} 1\ ,\ 9\ 8\ 7 \\ -\ 1\ ,\ 2\ 4\ 5 \\ \hline \end{array}$$

Answer: 7 4 2 miles

Example:

*Marianne took $53 with her to buy clothes. She spent $34. How much money did she have **left over**?*

The words *left over* tells us to subtract:

$$\begin{array}{r} \$\ 5\ 3 \\ -\ 3\ 4 \\ \hline \end{array}$$

Answer: $ 1 9 left over

Exercise 5-K

Find the *word* or *words* that tell us to subtract. Copy them before you solve the problems.

1. Jenny is 18 years old. Her grandfather is 78 years old. How much younger is Jenny than her grandfather?

2. A horse weighs 1,456 pounds. A dog weighs 47 pounds. What is the difference in their weights?

3. Paula's new car cost $8,500. Tammy's car cost $6,800. How much more did Paula pay than Tammy?

4. Joey Thatcher had $25 to spend. He bought a model car for $6, a football for $8, and a baseball bat for $9. How much money did he have left over?

5. Mr. and Mrs. Bowcott want to buy a television set. Television set A costs $175. Television set B costs $245. If they buy television set A, how much less will they pay?

Exercise 5-L   Problem Solving With Subtraction: BAKE SALE!

Raymond and his Math Club had a bake sale at school. They sold cakes, pies, doughnuts, and cookies.

How many sold?		How many sold?	
Chocolate doughnuts	38	Cherry pie	32 slices
Cinnamon doughnuts	45	Peach pie	24 slices
Sugar doughnuts	53	Apple pie	43 slices
Chocolate chip cookies	66	Lemon cake	16 slices
Peanut butter cookies	48	Chocolate cake	12 slices
Oatmeal cookies	55	Vanilla cake	14 slices

1. Compare the sugar doughnuts with the chocolate doughnuts. How many more sugar doughnuts did they sell?

2. Compare the cinnamon doughnuts with the chocolate doughnuts. How many more cinnamon doughnuts did they sell?

3. What kind of cookies did they sell the most?

4. The students made 80 chocolate chip cookies. How many were *not* sold?

5. The students made 32 slices of peach pie. How many slices of peach pie did they have *left over?*

6. How many slices of pie (cherry, peach, and apple) did they sell altogether?

7. The students made 40 slices of cherry pie, 50 slices of apple pie, and 32 slices of peach pie. How many slices of pie did they make altogether?

8. How many slices of pie were *left over?*

9. The students made 42 slices of cake (lemon, chocolate, and vanilla) altogether. How many slices of cake were *not* sold?

10. Did the Math Club sell more doughnuts or more cookies?

11. How many more?

Exercise 5-M   Problem Solving with Addition and Subtraction: HOCKEY!

NATIONAL HOCKEY LEAGUE

Team	Wins	Losses	Ties
Generals	11	4	0
Vikings	9	4	1
Lions	7	7	0
Eagles	6	8	1
Flyers	2	8	2

1. Which team has the most number of *wins?*

2. Which team has the least number of *wins?*

3. In what *place* (first, second, third, fourth, or fifth) is the Eagles?

4. How many *wins* does the second-place team have?

5. How many *losses* does the fourth-place team have?

6. Which team has more *losses:* the Lions or the Eagles?

7. Look at the *wins* for the Generals and the Flyers. How many more *wins* do the Generals have?

8. What are the total *wins* for all five teams?

9. Look at the *losses* for the Vikings and the Eagles. How many more *losses* do the Eagles have?

10. Do the Flyers have more *wins* or more *losses?*

11. How many more?

12. Look at the *wins* and *losses* for the Generals. How many more *wins* do they have?

13. Which two teams have 1 *tie* each?

14. Which team has the most *ties?*

Exercise 5-N   Problem Solving with Subtraction: BASKETBALL!

The North Hills High School basketball team played eight games last year:

Game	1	2	3	4	5	6	7	8
North Hills High scores	57	65	42	75	39	52	60	58
Opponent scores	48	73	48	60	64	45	51	32

1. Which games did North Hills High School *win?*

2. Which games did North Hills High School *lose?*

3. Look at game 2. What is the *point difference* between North Hills High and the opponent?

4. Look at game 3. What is the *point difference* between North Hills High and the opponent?

5. Look at game 5. What is the *point difference* between North Hills High and the opponent?

6. In which game (game 2, 3, or 5) is the point difference between North Hills High and the opponent the *greatest?*

7. In which game (game 2, 3, or 5) is the point difference between North Hills High and the opponent the *least?*

8. Look at the scores for the five games that North Hills High won. What is the *sum* of the scores?

9. Look at the opponents' scores for the same five games. What is the *sum* of their scores?

10. How many *more* points did North Hills High make for those five games?

11. Compare games 5 and 8. In which game (5 or 8) is the point difference *greater?*

12. Compare games 4 and 6. In which game (4 or 6) is the point difference *less?*

13. Look at all the games. Which two games have equal point differences?

Write with *words*.

1. 6 – 2 = 4
2. 15 – 5 = 10
3. 18 – 9 = 9

Complete.

4. 23 – 2 = 21   Minuend: ___   Subtrahend: ___   Difference: ___

Use the inverse operation to find the missing numbers:

5. 17 + ___ = 123
6. ___ + 201 = 342
7. ___ – 344 = 536

Subtract.

8. 76 – 15	13. 243 – 189	18. 200 – 175
9. 55 – 32	14. 543 – 289	19. 350 – 286
10. 278 – 132	15. 2,133 – 1,967	20. 1,200 – 388
11. 788 – 254	16. 123,834 – 2,875	21. 6,002 – 5,988
12. 34 – 27	17. 301 – 167	22. 354,000 – 276,988

23. Sarah bought three dozen eggs. While she was driving home, 17 eggs broke. How many eggs did she have left over?

24. Kim got 45 on her math test. Terry got 57. How many more points did Terry get than Kim?

25. John is eighteen years old. John's age is three years less than Peter's age and five years more than Paul's age. How old is:

a. Peter?   b. Paul?

6 Multiplication

6-1 Language of Multiplication

This is a **multiplication** problem:

$$4 \times 3 = 12$$

We say: "Four times three equals twelve."

The *product* is 12. The *factors* are 4 and 3.

What is the *product* of 5 and 2?

The product of 5 and 2 is 10.

Exercise 6-A

Complete each sentence:

1. The __product__ of six and two is twelve.
2. Eight _____ two equals sixteen.
3. The product of four and four is _____.
4. Nine times two _____ eighteen.
5. Six _____ six _____ thirty-six.
6. The _____ of eight and three _____ twenty- four.
7. _____ times seven _____ twenty-one.
8. The product of _____ and five is fifteen.
9. Five _____ nine _____ forty-five.
10. Four times _____ equals thirty-six.

Answer each question.

11. What is the product of four and five?   *twenty*
12. What is the product of nine and nine?
13. What is the product of eight and six?
14. What is the product of seven and nine?
15. What is the product of five and zero?

16. What is the product of three and nine?

17. What is the product of six and seven?

18. What is the product of seven and seven?

19. What is the product of two and four?

20. What is the product of eight and one?

Write with *words*.

21. $4 \times 3 = 12$ *Four times three equals twelve* or
                          The product of four and three is twelve.

22. $9 \times 2 = 18$

23. $8 \times 4 = 32$

24. $2 \times 6 = 12$

25. $1 \times 10 = 10$

26. $7 \times 5 = 35$

27. $9 \times 4 = 36$

28. $8 \times 5 = 40$

29. $6 \times 7 = 42$

30. $5 \times 4 = 20$

Complete.

31. $6 \times 8 = 48$ Factors: ___ and ___   Product: ___

32. $9 \times 0 = 0$ Factors: ___ and ___   Product: ___

33. $8 \times 7 = 56$ Factors: ___ and ___   Product: ___

34. $6 \times 9 = 54$ Factors: ___ and ___   Product: ___

6-2   Symbols for Multiplication

We can write multiplication problems in different ways:

$$4 \times 3 \text{ or } 4 \cdot 3 \text{ or } (4)(3) \text{ or } 4(3) \text{ or } (4)3$$

Exercise 6-B

Write each multiplication problem in two more ways.

1. 6×2 3. $(9)(4)$ 5. $8 \cdot 4 \cdot 2$

2. $5 \cdot 3$ 4. 14×2 6. $6(3)(2)$

7. $(4 + 6)2$

8. $25 \times 3 \times 2$

9. $(18)4$

10. $11 \times (9 \cdot 6)$

11. $12(2 + 4)$

12. $(4 + 3) \cdot (2 + 8)$

6-3 Commutative Property of Multiplication

Look at the following:

$$2 \cdot 5 = 10 \qquad 5 \cdot 2 = 10$$

The products are equal.

$$2 \cdot 5 = 5 \cdot 2$$

The *order* of multiplying numbers does not change the product.

COMMUTATIVE PROPERTY OF MULTIPLICATION:

We can multiply numbers in any order. For all numbers a and b:

$$a \cdot b = b \cdot a$$

6-4 Associative Property of Multiplication

We can group $2 \cdot 3 \cdot 4$ in these ways:

$$(2 \cdot 3)\, 4 = \qquad 2\, (3 \cdot 4) =$$

$$(6)\quad 4 = 24 \qquad 2\, (12) = 24$$

The products are equal.

ASSOCIATIVE PROPERTY OF MULTIPLICATION:

If we group three or more numbers in different ways and multiply them together, the product does not change. For all numbers a, b, and c:

$$(a \cdot b)\, c = a\, (b \cdot c)$$

6-5 Multiplicative Identity Property of Multiplication

$$4 \cdot 1 = 4$$

$$17 \cdot 1 = 17$$

MULTIPLICATIVE IDENTITY PROPERTY OF MULTIPLICATION:

Multiplying any number by 1 does not change the value of the number. For all numbers a:

$$a \cdot 1 = a$$

6-6 | Multiplicative Property of Zero

$$6 \cdot 0 = 0$$
$$23 \cdot 0 = 0$$

MULTIPLICATIVE PROPERTY OF ZERO:

Multiplying any number by zero makes the product zero. For all numbers a:

$$a \cdot 0 = 0$$

What does it mean to multiply a number by zero? Look at the example:

Example:

Notebooks cost $2 each. 3 notebooks cost $2 × 3 = $6
2 notebooks cost $2 × 2 = $4
0 notebooks cost $2 × 0 = $0

Exercise 6-C

Fill in the numbers, then write the property shown: commutative, associative, multiplicative identity, or multiplicative property of zero.

1. $4 \cdot 2 = 2 \cdot 4$ <u>Commutative</u>

2. $16 \cdot 1 = $ ___   _____

3. $(8 \cdot 3)$ ___ $= 8(3 \cdot 4)$ _____

4. $95 = 95 \cdot$ ___   _____

5. $19(4 \cdot 2) = 19(2 \cdot$ ___$)$ _____

6. $(11 \cdot 4)0 = $ ___   _____

7. $1 \cdot m = $ ___   _____

8. $(9 \cdot m)n = $ ___ $(m \cdot n)$ _____

9. $p \cdot$ ___ $= 0$ _____

10. $11(6 \cdot r) = 11(\_\_ \cdot 6)$ _____

11. $12 \cdot 0 = \_\_ \cdot 12$ _____

12. $s \cdot \_\_ = s$ _____

13. $a(b)0 = \_\_$ _____

14. $(4 \cdot p) \cdot \_\_ = c(4 \cdot p)$ _____

15. $b(c \cdot d) = (b \cdot c)\_\_$ _____

6-7 Distributive Property of Multiplication

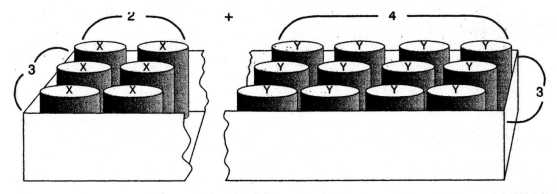

Altogether, there are $3(2 + 4) = 18$ cans. There are $3 \cdot 2 = 6x$ cans and $3 \cdot 4 = 12y$ cans. So:

$$3(2 + 4) = 3 \cdot 2 + 3 \cdot 4$$
$$3(6) \ = \ 6 \ + \ 12$$

This is an example of the **distributive property**.

$$
\begin{array}{cc}
3 & + & 2 \\
\end{array}
$$

Altogether, there are $4(3 + 2)$ circles. There are $4 \cdot 3$ black circles and $4 \cdot 2$ white circles. So:

$$4(3 + 2) = 4 \cdot 3 + 4 \cdot 2$$
$$4(5) = \ 12 \ + \ 8$$

DISTRIBUTIVE PROPERTY OF MULTIPLICATION:

For all numbers a, b, and c:

$$a(b + c) = a \cdot b + a \cdot c$$

Use the distributive property to complete the following.

1. $8(2 + 4) = (8 \cdot 2) + (8 \cdot 4) = 16 + 32 = 48$
2. $3(4 + 1) =$.
3. $9(6 + 2) =$
4. $a(b + c) =$
5. $(40 + 20)5 =$
6. $7(m + n) =$
7. $(6 \cdot 3) + (6 \cdot 2) =$
8. $(9 \cdot 7) + (3 \cdot 7) =$
9. $(4 \cdot 11) + (5 \cdot 11) =$
10. $(x \cdot 9) + (x \cdot 4) =$
11. $3(m + n) =$
12. $(15 \cdot 12) + (15 \cdot 13) =$
13. $(r \cdot x) + (r \cdot y) =$
14. $p(t + s) =$
15. $(4 \cdot 190) + (4 \cdot 190) =$

6-8 Multiplying Two-Digit and Three-Digit Numbers by a One-Digit Number

Example:
```
  1 3
×   2
```

Multiply the numbers in the ones' place: $3 \times 2 = 6$. Write the 6 in the ones' place.

```
  1 3
×   2
    6
```

Multiply the 1 in the tens' place by the 2 in the ones' place: $1 \times 2 = 2$. Write the 2 in the tens' place.

```
  1 3
×   2
  2 6
```

Example:

$$\begin{array}{r} 2\ 3\ 1 \\ \times \qquad 3 \\ \hline \end{array}$$

Multiply the 1 in the ones' place by 3: $1 \times 3 = 3$.

$$\begin{array}{r} 2\ 3\ 1 \\ \times \qquad 3 \\ \hline 3 \end{array}$$

Multiply the 3 in the tens' place by 3: $3 \times 3 = 9$.

$$\begin{array}{r} 2\ 3\ 1 \\ \times \qquad 3 \\ \hline 9\ 3 \end{array}$$

Multiply the 2 in the hundreds' place by 3: $2 \times 3 = 6$.

$$\begin{array}{r} 2\ 3\ 1 \\ \times \qquad 3 \\ \hline 6\ 9\ 3 \end{array}$$

Exercise 6-E

Multiply the following numbers.

1. $\begin{array}{r} 13 \\ \times\ 3 \\ \hline \end{array}$	7. $\begin{array}{r} 44 \\ \times\ 2 \\ \hline \end{array}$	13. $\begin{array}{r} 64 \\ \times\ 2 \\ \hline \end{array}$	19. $\begin{array}{r} 543 \\ \times\ 2 \\ \hline \end{array}$
2. $\begin{array}{r} 42 \\ \times\ 3 \\ \hline \end{array}$	8. $\begin{array}{r} 14 \\ \times\ 2 \\ \hline \end{array}$	14. $\begin{array}{r} 221 \\ \times\ 2 \\ \hline \end{array}$	20. $\begin{array}{r} 421 \\ \times\ 3 \\ \hline \end{array}$
3. $\begin{array}{r} 51 \\ \times\ 6 \\ \hline \end{array}$	9. $\begin{array}{r} 42 \\ \times\ 4 \\ \hline \end{array}$	15. $\begin{array}{r} 142 \\ \times\ 2 \\ \hline \end{array}$	21. $\begin{array}{r} 213 \\ \times\ 3 \\ \hline \end{array}$
4. $\begin{array}{r} 33 \\ \times\ 3 \\ \hline \end{array}$	10. $\begin{array}{r} 63 \\ \times\ 2 \\ \hline \end{array}$	16. $\begin{array}{r} 323 \\ \times\ 3 \\ \hline \end{array}$	22. $\begin{array}{r} 112 \\ \times\ 4 \\ \hline \end{array}$
5. $\begin{array}{r} 24 \\ \times\ 2 \\ \hline \end{array}$	11. $\begin{array}{r} 83 \\ \times\ 3 \\ \hline \end{array}$	17. $\begin{array}{r} 443 \\ \times\ 2 \\ \hline \end{array}$	23. $\begin{array}{r} 203 \\ \times\ 2 \\ \hline \end{array}$
6. $\begin{array}{r} 23 \\ \times\ 2 \\ \hline \end{array}$	12. $\begin{array}{r} 21 \\ \times\ 9 \\ \hline \end{array}$	18. $\begin{array}{r} 133 \\ \times\ 3 \\ \hline \end{array}$	24. $\begin{array}{r} 231 \\ \times\ 3 \\ \hline \end{array}$

Example: 5 6
                 ×   7

Multiply 6 × 7. The product is 42. We can only write one number in the ones' place, so we write the 2 in the ones' place and carry the 4.

$$\begin{array}{r} 4 \\ 5\ 6 \\ \times\quad 7 \\ \hline 2 \end{array}$$

Multiply 5 × 7. The product is 35. We add the 4 that we carried: 35 + 4 = 39.

$$\begin{array}{r} 4 \\ 5\ 6 \\ \times\quad 7 \\ \hline 3\ 9\ 2 \end{array}$$

Example: 3 0 6
                 ×   5

Multiply 6 × 5. The product is 30. Write the 0 in the one's place and carry the 3 to the tens' place digit.

$$\begin{array}{r} 3 \\ 3\ 0\ 6 \\ \times\quad\ \ 5 \\ \hline 0 \end{array}$$

Multiply 0 × 5. The product is 0. Add the 3 that we carried: 0 + 3 = 3. Write the 3 in the tens' place.

$$\begin{array}{r} 3 \\ 3\ 0\ 6 \\ \times\quad\ \ 5 \\ \hline 3\ 0 \end{array}$$

Multiply 3 × 5. The product is 15.

$$\begin{array}{r} 3 \\ 3\ 0\ 6 \\ \times\quad\ \ 5 \\ \hline 1\ 5\ 3\ 0 \end{array}$$

Exercise 6-F

Multiply the following numbers.

1.	36 × 4	3.	44 × 3	5.	66 × 8	7.	42 × 9
2.	56 × 7	4.	72 × 8	6.	87 × 9	8.	15 × 6

9. 59 × 9	15. 85 × 5	21. 734 × 5	27. 832 × 9
10. 67 × 4	16. 467 × 6	22. 509 × 6	28. 208 × 3
11. 25 × 4	17. 294 × 3	23. 921 × 3	29. 874 × 8
12. 67 × 3	18. 908 × 5	24. 565 × 7	30. 620 × 6
13. 53 × 7	19. 385 × 7	25. 988 × 6	31. 944 × 7
14. 88 × 9	20. 538 × 8	26. 734 × 2	32. 802 × 8

6-10   Multiplying Two Digits by Two Digits

Example:

$$\begin{array}{r} 2\ 1 \\ \times\ 3\ 4 \end{array}$$

First, multiply 21 × 4. This will be *product A*.
(21 × 4 = 84.)

$$\begin{array}{r} 2\ 1 \\ \times\ 3\ 4 \\ \hline \end{array}$$

product A →   8 4

Next, multiply 21 × 3. This will be *product B*.
(21 × 3 = 63.) Write the 3 in the tens' place since we are multiplying 3 tens times 1 ones.

$$\begin{array}{r} 2\ 1 \\ \times\ 3\ 4 \\ \hline \end{array}$$

product A →   8 4
product B →   6 3

Add *product A* and *product B* together. The sum will be the answer.

$$\begin{array}{r} 2\ 1 \\ \times\ 3\ 4 \\ \hline \end{array}$$

product A →   8 4
product B →   6 3
Answer →   7 1 4

Multiply the following numbers.

1.	32 × 22	6.	83 × 12	11.	20 × 34	16.	45 × 11
2.	31 × 24	7.	92 × 13	12.	52 × 14	17.	50 × 23
3.	42 × 13	8.	54 × 22	13.	43 × 33	18.	44 × 22
4.	63 × 23	9.	33 × 33	14.	62 × 40	19.	61 × 24
5.	72 × 14	10.	42 × 23	15.	73 × 22	20.	53 × 30

6-11 Multiplying Two-Digit Numbers by Two-Digit Numbers with Carrying

Example:
$$\begin{array}{r} 6\ 7 \\ \times\ 2\ 8 \end{array}$$

First, multiply 7 × 8. Carry the 5 above the 6 in the tens' place. Multiply 6 × 8 and add the 5 that we carried. This will be *product A*.

$$\begin{array}{r} \overset{5}{6}\ 7 \\ \times\ 2\ 8 \\ \hline \end{array}$$
product A → 5 3 6

Next, multiply 7 × 2. Write the 4 in the tens' place and carry the 1 to the hundreds'. Multiply 6 × 2 and add the 1 that we carried. This will be *product B*.

$$\begin{array}{r} \overset{1}{6}\ 7 \\ \times\ 2\ 8 \\ \hline \end{array}$$
product A → 5 3 6
product B → 1 3 4

Add *product A* and *product B* together. The sum will be the answer.

$$\begin{array}{r} 6\ 7 \\ \times\ 2\ 8 \\ \hline \end{array}$$
product A → 5 3 6
product B → + 1 3 4
Answer → 1 8 7 6

Multiply the following numbers:

1. 34
    × 24

2. 45
    × 56

3. 53
    × 27

4. 73
    × 92

5. 26
    × 19

6. 76
    × 87

7. 93
    × 55

8. 81
    × 83

9. 13
    × 34

10. 77
    × 64

11. 82
    × 44

12. 63
    × 77

13. 92
    × 23

14. 75
    × 75

15. 55
    × 44

16. 32
    × 99

17. 29
    × 99

18. 28
    × 28

19. 35
    × 35

20. 99
    × 99

21. 45
    × 36

22. 84
    × 48

23. 23
    × 90

24. 64
    × 69

25. 89
    × 90

26. 35
    × 78

27. 66
    × 33

28. 59
    × 60

29. 91
    × 19

30. 44
    × 78

31. 63
    × 99

32. 49
    × 12

6-12 Multiplying Three-Digit Numbers by Two- and Three-Digit Numbers

Example: 2 3 4
         ×   6 3

First, multiply 234 × 3. This will be *product A*.

                              2 3 4
                        ×   6 3
         product A →   7 0 2

Next, multiply 234 × 6. This will be *product B*.

                              2 3 4
                        ×   6 3
         product A →   7 0 2
         product B →   1 4 0 4

Add *product A* and *product B* for the answer.

$$
\begin{array}{r}
2\ 3\ 4 \\
\times\ \ \ \ 6\ 3 \\
\hline
\end{array}
$$

product A →   7 0 2
product B → 1 4 0 4
Answer → 1 4 7 4 2

Example:
$$
\begin{array}{r}
3\ 6\ 5 \\
\times\ \ 2\ 4\ 3 \\
\hline
\end{array}
$$

First, multiply 365 × 3 (*product A*). Next, multiply 365 × 4 (*product B*). Then multiply 365 × 2 (*product C*). Add *products A*, *B*, and *C* together for the answer.

$$
\begin{array}{r}
3\ 6\ 5 \\
\times\ \ 2\ 4\ 3 \\
\hline
\end{array}
$$

product A → 1 0 9 5
product B → 1 4 6 0
product C →   7 3 0
Answer → 8 8 6 9 5

Exercise 6-1

Multiply the following numbers.

1. 342 × 25	9. 904 × 83	17. 790 ×459	25. 900 ×432
2. 980 × 34	10. 592 × 56	18. 889 ×347	26. 387 ×102
3. 546 × 49	11. 722 × 45	19. 506 ×677	27. 566 ×143
4. 688 × 55	12. 609 × 69	20. 622 ×678	28. 760 ×301
5. 732 × 99	13. 344 × 78	21. 403 ×344	29. 311 ×100
6. 937 × 57	14. 922 × 88	22. 322 ×498	30. 986 ×288
7. 258 × 96	15. 811 × 55	23. 123 ×123	31. 598 ×385
8. 522 × 66	16. 604 ×435	24. 865 ×302	32. 290 ×307

DEFINITION: Multiple of Ten

A *multiple of ten* is the product of 10 with any number:

$2 \times 10 = 20$	$5 \times 10 = 50$	$8 \times 10 = 80$	$11 \times 10 = 110$
$3 \times 10 = 30$	$6 \times 10 = 60$	$9 \times 10 = 90$	$12 \times 10 = 120$
$4 \times 10 = 40$	$7 \times 10 = 70$	$10 \times 10 = 100$	$13 \times 10 = 130$

(20, 30, 40, 50, 60, 70, 80, 90, 100, 110, 120, 130, . . . are all *multiples of ten*.)

$$100 \times 10 = 1,000$$
$$1,000 \times 10 = 10,000$$
$$10,000 \times 10 = 100,000$$

(1,000, 10,000, 100,000 . . . are also *multiples of ten*.)

To multiply a number by a *multiple of ten*, we multiply the *nonzero* digits and combine the zeros.

Example:

$$100 \times 1,000$$

Multiply 1×1: 1×1 $= 1$

Combine the zeros: 2 zeros and 3 zeros = 5 zeros

Answer: **100,000**

1 and 5 zeros

Example:

$$30 \times 100$$

Multiply 3×1: 3×1 $= 3$

Combine the zeros: 1 zero and 2 zeros = 3 zeros

Answer: **3,000**

3 and 3 zeros

Example:

$$74 \times 20 \times 1,000$$
$$\uparrow \quad \uparrow \quad \uparrow$$

Multiply $74 \times 2 \times 1$: $74 \times 2 \times 1 \quad = 148$

Combine the zeros: 1 zero and 3 zeros = 4 zeros

Answer: 1,480,000
        $\uparrow$
148 and 4 zeros

Exercise 6-J

Multiply.

1. 6×100
2. $24 \times 10,000$
3. 100×76
4. $10 \times 10,000$
5. $2,743 \times 10,000$
6. $1,000 \times 1,000$
7. $100 \times 3,450$
8. $2,300 \times 1,000$
9. $10 \times 100 \times 678$
10. $1,000 \times 890 \times 100$
11. $387,000 \times 1,000,000$
12. $65,000 \times 10 \times 1,000$

13. $1,000 \times 30 \times 300$
14. $1,000 \times 300 \times 20$
15. $450 \times 2,000,000$
16. $10 \times 60,000 \times 200$
17. $107,233 \times 10 \times 100$
18. $200 \times 14,000 \times 2,000$
19. $134 \times 3,000 \times 100$
20. $456,000 \times 300 \times 20,000$
21. $1,000 \times 40,000 \times 23,000$
22. $70,000 \times 400 \times 2,000,000$
23. $25,000 \times 300 \times 2,000,000$
24. $80,000 \times 2,000 \times 1,000 \times 200$

6-14   Word Problems with Unnecessary Information

Some problems in math have *unnecessary* information. We don't need this unnecessary information to solve problems.

It is *necessary* to listen in class.

It is *unnecessary* to talk in class.

It is *necessary* to study after school.

It is *unnecessary* to watch TV after school.

Example:

John sold four paintings at the Art Fair. He sold each painting for $125. It took John 6 months to paint each one. How much money did he make on the sales?

Unnecessary information: "It took John 6 months to paint each one." We don't need this information to solve the problem. We want to know *how much money* he made.

Answer: $125 × 4 paintings = $500

Exercise 6-K

Which information is *unnecessary*?

1. Matthew collects baseball cards. He has 2,565 cards in all. He sold 35 cards last month for $5 each. How much money did he make?
   a. He has 2,565 cards in all.
   b. He sold 35 cards last month.
   c. He sold the cards for $5 each.

2. Reina was born in 1973. She graduated from high school when she was 18 years old. She has lived in New York for 10 years. In what year did she graduate?
   a. Reina was born in 1973.
   b. She graduated from high school when she was 18 years old.
   c. She has lived in New York for 10 years.

3. Jasmine drove 35 miles an hour. She drove for 5 hours. She rested for 2 hours. How far did she drive?
   a. Jasmine drove 35 miles an hour.
   b. She drove for 5 hours.
   c. She rested for 2 hours.

4. Linda is 15 years old. She is 6 years older than her brother. Her father is 25 years older than Linda. How old is her brother?
   a. Linda is 15 years old.
   b. She is 6 years older than her brother.
   c. Her father is 25 years older than Linda.

5. Michael began painting the house at 9:00 A.M. He finished one half of the house at 2:00 P.M. He finished painting the house at 6:00 P.M. How many hours did he paint that day?
   a. Michael began painting the house at 9:00 A.M.
   b. He finished one half of the house at 2:00 P.M.
   c. He finished painting the house at 6:00 P.M.

6. Franklin School has 2,507 students. Fairfield School has 545 more students than Franklin School. Both schools have 115 teachers. How many more students than teachers does Franklin School have?
   a. Franklin School has 2,507 students.
   b. Fairfield School has 545 more students than Franklin School.
   c. Both schools have 115 teachers.

6-15 Solving Multiplication Word Problems

Example:

Daisy works after school at "Clothes For You." Her salary is $6 an hour. In 2 days, she worked 8 hours. What was her pay?

Multiplication is a fast way to add. We can solve this problem by:

Addition: $\underbrace{\$6 + \$6 + \$6 + \$6 + \$6 + \$6 + \$6 + \$6}_{\text{for 8 hours}} = \$48$

or

Multiplication: $\$6 \times 8 \text{ hours} = \$48$

Multiplication is faster than addition.

Example:

> *Morgan's salary is $300 a month. Oliver's salary is **three times** Morgan's salary. What is Oliver's salary?*

The words *three times* tells us that we can multiply:

$$\$300 \times 3 = \$900$$

Exercise 6-L

Use only the *necessary* information to solve each problem:

1. Tam Li was born in 1978. He has lived in the United States for 15 years. How old was he in 1990?

2. Lisa loves to read. She reads 20 pages in 1 hour. Her favorite book has 270 pages. How many pages does she read in 6 hours?

3. Henry paints cars. He paints 16 cars a month. He asks $350 for each car he paints. How much does he earn by painting 7 cars?

4. A watermelon has 175 seeds. Each watermelon is 18 inches long. How many seeds do 5 watermelons have?

5. The Humane Society has 23 dogs, 15 cats, and 5 birds. The birds and cats are free, but the dogs cost $20 each. How many animals are there altogether?

6. Brandon began studying at 4:00 P.M. He finished 2 pages of math, 3 pages of English, and 1 page of biology. He studied for 4 hours. What time did he stop studying?

7. An artist finished 1 painting in 7 months. He began in February. He painted 5 hours a week. How many hours did he paint altogether during the 7 months?

8. Scott runs 4 miles every weekday (Monday through Friday). He does not run on Saturday or Sunday. He runs 35 minutes a day. How many miles does he run in 4 weeks?

9. Maria invited 18 friends to her party. Each person brought 1 friend. There were 17 boys. How many people were at her party, including Maria?

10. Gregory earns $25 a week. He saves $9 a week. How much does he earn in 6 weeks?

Raymond Lopez works after school at The Pizza Pan restaurant. He is a waiter. Look at his weekly work schedule:

Monday	Tuesday	Wednesday	Thursday	Friday	Saturday
5 hr	4 hr	6 hr	5 hr	6 hr	8 hr

1. When Raymond began work as a waiter there, his hourly wage was $6 an hour. How much did he earn:

   a. on Wednesday?   c. on Tuesday?   e. on Friday?
   b. on Monday?   d. on Saturday?   f. in one week?

2. How much did Raymond earn in 1 month? (There are 4 weeks in a month.)

3. How much did Raymond earn in 6 months?

4. Sometimes, Raymond worked *overtime* (working more than 8 hours in one day). When he worked *overtime*, he received $3 more for each hour of overtime. One Saturday, Raymond worked 12 hours. How much did he earn that day?

5. Later, Raymond received a raise (higher hourly wage) of $2 more an hour. What was his *new* hourly wage?

6. How much did Raymond earn in 1 *week* with his raise?

7. How much did he earn in 1 *month* with his raise?

8. Compare Raymond's weekly salary before and after his raise. How much *more* did he earn per week with his raise?

9. How much *more* did he earn per month with his raise?

The Nelson family traveled to Japan last month. Mr. and Mrs. Nelson traveled with their two children, Rick, age 16, and Lisa, age 14.

1. Japanese money is called *yen*. If 1 American dollar is equal to 125 Japanese *yen*, how much would each of the following items cost in Japan?

	United States	Japan
a. a cup of coffee	$1	____ yen
b. dinner for one person	$8	____ yen
c. a watch	$60	____ yen
d. a camera	$130	____ yen
e. a cassette player	$230	____ yen
f. a television set	$350	____ yen
g. a new car	$12,000	____ yen

2. The Nelsons stayed at Cherry Hotel in Tokyo. The cost for one night was 8,125 yen. How much did they pay for 2 weeks in yen?

3. Food in Japan is expensive! For lunch one day, Rick ordered a hamburger for 750 yen. Lisa ordered a ham sandwich for 875 yen. Mrs. Nelson ordered a salad for 1,250 yen, and Mr. Nelson ordered a steak sandwich for 1,500 yen. Mr. Nelson gave the waitress 6,000 yen. How much change in *yen* did he receive?

4. Mrs. Nelson went shopping in Tokyo and in Kyoto. She saw a dress for sale. In Tokyo, the dress cost 7,625 yen. In Kyoto, the same dress cost 58 dollars.
   a. Which was *cheaper*, the dress in Tokyo for 7,625 yen or the dress in Kyoto for 58 dollars?
   b. How much cheaper, in *yen*?

5. Mr. and Mrs. Nelson wanted to rent a car to see the country. The children wanted to take the Bullet Train. Look at the cost for car and train and see which is cheaper:

Rent a Car	**Bullet Train**
Car for 1 *day:* 4,375 yen	1 *adult* ticket for 1 *week:* 5,000 yen
Car for 1 *week:* 17,500 yen	1 *student* ticket for 1 *week:* 2,500 yen

a. If the Nelsons rent a car for *2 weeks*, how much will they pay in yen?

b. If the Nelsons buy train tickets for each person in the family for *2 weeks*, how much will they pay in yen? (Rick and Lisa are students.)

c. Which is *cheaper* for the *2* weeks, renting a car or taking a train?

d. How much cheaper, in yen?

6. If the Nelsons paid $2,300 for airplane tickets for all four family members, how much is this in Japanese yen?

7. What is the *total* amount they spent in yen on airplane tickets, hotel, and train tickets for *2 weeks?*

LET'S TALK ABOUT ...

1. multiplication
2. factor
3. product
4. times
5. multiplicative identity property
6. multiplicative property of zero
7. distributive property

8. multiple of ten
9. carry
10. necessary information
11. unnecessary information
12. hourly wage
13. overtime
14. cheaper

Write with words.

1. $7 \times 10 = 70$
2. $3 \times 5 = 15$
3. $9 \times 8 = 72$

Multiply by combining zeros.

4. $10,000 \times 1,000$
5. $100 \times 5,000 \times 600$
6. $70,000 \times 40 \times 5,000$

Complete.

7. $15 \times 3 = 45$ Factors: ___ and ___   Product: ___

Multiply.

8. 7×7
9. 6×5
10. 3×13
11. 23×2
12. 76×6

13. 55×7
14. 534×9
15. 874×4
16. 23×45
17. 75×94

18. 86×52
19. 245×98
20. 603×95
21. 576×984
22. 366×843

23. Harry can throw a football 36 feet. His brother, Wills, can throw a football twice (two times) as far. How far can Wills throw a football?

24. Megan weighs 92 pounds. Her father's weight is three times Megan's weight. Her brother's weight is twice Megan's weight.
    a. How much does her brother weigh?
    b. How much does Megan's father weigh?
    c. How much do all three people weigh altogether?

25. Monte Vista Theater is selling tickets to their play. The "A" tickets cost $20 per person. The "B" tickets cost $15 per person, and the "C" tickets cost $12 per person. Last month the theater sold 350 "A" tickets, 489 "B" tickets, and 593 "C" tickets.
    a. How much money did they receive from "A" tickets only?
    b. How much money did they receive from "B" tickets only?
    c. How much money did they receive from "C" tickets only?
    d. How much money did they receive altogether?

26. This number has five digits:

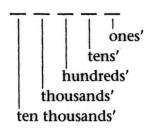
ones'
tens'
hundreds'
thousands'
ten thousands'

The ten thousands' digit is 2. The thousands' digit is three times the ten thousands digit. The hundreds' digit is two more than the thousands' digit. The tens' digit is 7 less than the hundreds' digit. The ones' digit is twice the tens' digit. What is the number?

7 Division

7-1 Language of Division

This is a **division** problem:

$$10 \div 2 = 5$$
We say: "Ten divided by two equals five."

The *quotient* is five. The *dividend* is ten. The *divisor* is two.

What is the *quotient* of 6 and 2?

The quotient of 6 and 2 is 3.

Exercise 7-A

Complete each sentence.

1. The _quotient_ of eight and four is two.
2. Twenty-four _____ three _____ eight.
3. The quotient of _____ and eight is three.
4. Twelve _____ six equals two.
5. Thirty-six _____ four _____ nine.
6. Nine divided by three _____ three.
7. The quotient of twelve and three is _____.
8. The _____ of forty-two and seven _____ six.
9. _____ divided by seven _____seven.
10. Fifty-four _____ nine _____ six.

Answer the questions.

11. What is the quotient of nine and three?   *three*
12. What is the quotient of forty and eight?
13. What is the quotient of thirty and five?
14. What is the quotient of twenty-one and three?
15. What is the quotient of sixteen and two?

16. What is the quotient of forty-five and five?

17. What is the quotient of twenty-seven and nine?

18. What is the quotient of eighteen and three?

19. What is the quotient of fifteen and fifteen?

20. What is the quotient of nineteen and one?

Write with words.

21. $12 \div 6 = 2$ *Twelve divided by six equals two* or
    The quotient of twelve and six is two.

22. $15 \div 5 = 3$

23. $14 \div 7 = 2$

24. $9 \div 9 = 1$

25. $35 \div 7 = 5$

26. $49 \div 7 = 7$

27. $24 \div 3 = 8$

28. $63 \div 7 = 9$

29. $64 \div 8 = 8$

30. $42 \div 7 = 6$

Complete.

31. $20 \div 10 = 2$ Dividend: ___   Divisor: ___   Quotient: ___

32. $16 \div 8 = 2$ Dividend: ___   Divisor: ___   Quotient: ___

33. $35 \div 7 = 5$ Dividend: ___   Divisor: ___   Quotient: ___

34. $12 \div 4 = 3$ Dividend: ___   Divisor: ___   Quotient: ___

35. $18 \div 9 = 2$ Dividend: ___   Divisor: ___   Quotient: ___

7-2 Dividing with One-Digit Divisors

We write division problems with the symbol $\div$ or $\overline{)}$. We write "eight divided by four" as:

$$8 \div 4 \quad \text{or} \quad 4\overline{)8}$$

In the problem above, we want to know how many *times* 4 goes into 8. We can use *multiplication* to find the quotient:

$$4 \times \underline{\ ?\ } = 8$$
$$4 \times \underline{\ 2\ } = 8$$

4 goes into 8 *two times*. The quotient is 2.
Write the quotient 2 above the dividend 8:

$$\begin{array}{r} 2 \\ 4{\overline{\smash{\big)}\,8}} \end{array}$$

Multiply the divisor 4 times the quotient 2: $4 \times 2 = 8$.
Write the product 8 below the dividend and subtract
it from the dividend.

$$\begin{array}{r} 2 \\ 4{\overline{\smash{\big)}\,8}} \\ \underline{-8} \\ 0 \end{array}$$

To check your answer, multiply the divisor (4)
with the quotient (2). The product should equal
the dividend (8).

quotient		2
$\times$ divisor		$\times\ 4$
dividend		8

Example: $4{\overline{\smash{\big)}\,24}}$

$4 \times ? = 2$. 2 is too small. We must use 24.
$4 \times ? = 24$. $4 \times 6 = 24$.
Write the quotient 6 above the 4, not the 2,
because we are using 24, not 2.

$$\begin{array}{r} 6 \\ 4{\overline{\smash{\big)}\,24}} \\ \underline{-24} \\ 0 \end{array}$$

Check your answer:

$$\begin{array}{r} 6 \\ \times\ 4 \\ \hline 24 \end{array}$$

Example: $4{\overline{\smash{\big)}\,636}}$

$4 \times ? = 6$. $4 \times 1 = 4$. $4 \times 2 = 8$. 2 is too large. Use 1.
Write it above the 6, multiply 1×4, and subtract it
from 6.

Bring down the 3.

$$\begin{array}{r} 1 \\ 4{\overline{\smash{\big)}\,636}} \\ \underline{-\ 4} \\ 23 \end{array}$$

$4 \times ? = 23$. $4 \times 5 = 20$. $4 \times 6 = 24$. Use 5. Write 5
above the 3 and multiply 4×5. Write the product
20 below 23 and subtract.

Bring down the 6.

$$\begin{array}{r} 15 \\ 4{\overline{\smash{\big)}\,636}} \\ \underline{-\ 4} \\ 23 \\ \underline{-\ 20} \\ 36 \end{array}$$

$4 \times ? = 36.$ $4 \times 9 = 36.$ Write the 9 above the 6.
Multiply 4×9 and subtract from 36.

The *quotient*, or *answer*, is 159.

$$\begin{array}{r} 159 \\ 4\overline{)636} \\ -\underline{4} \\ 23 \\ -\underline{20} \\ 36 \\ -\underline{36} \\ 0 \end{array}$$

Check your answer:

$$\begin{array}{r} 159 \\ \times4 \\ \hline 636 \end{array}$$

Exercise 7-B

Divide and check your answers.

1. $2\overline{)6}$ 6. $7\overline{)14}$ 11. $2\overline{)34}$

2. $5\overline{)45}$ 7. $5\overline{)10}$ 12. $4\overline{)84}$

3. $6\overline{)24}$ 8. $9\overline{)72}$ 13. $7\overline{)77}$

4. $3\overline{)9}$ 9. $8\overline{)56}$ 14. $2\overline{)46}$

5. $2\overline{)8}$ 10. $3\overline{)99}$ 15. $5\overline{)55}$

Divide.

16. $8\overline{)648}$ 21. $4\overline{)444}$ 26. $7\overline{)308}$

17. $3\overline{)243}$ 22. $2\overline{)646}$ 27. $8\overline{)176}$

18. $7\overline{)105}$ 23. $3\overline{)552}$ 28. $9\overline{)792}$

19. $8\overline{)152}$ 24. $4\overline{)252}$ 29. $8\overline{)440}$

20. $6\overline{)150}$ 25. $3\overline{)198}$ 30. $6\overline{)366}$

91

Divide.

31. $2\overline{)4568}$ 36. $3\overline{)1941}$ 41. $4\overline{)1476}$

32. $3\overline{)1533}$ 37. $2\overline{)3196}$ 42. $9\overline{)2043}$

33. $5\overline{)3550}$ 38. $9\overline{)1944}$ 43. $4\overline{)1064}$

34. $4\overline{)6184}$ 39. $6\overline{)1536}$ 44. $7\overline{)5768}$

35. $9\overline{)1584}$ 40. $6\overline{)1308}$ 45. $3\overline{)7731}$

Example: $6\overline{)12012}$

$6 \times ? = 12$. $6 \times 2 = 12$. Write the 2 above the 2, multiply and subtract. Bring down the 0.

$$
\begin{array}{r}
2 \\
6{\overline{\smash{)}\,12012}} \\
\underline{-\ 12} \\
00
\end{array}
$$

$6 \times ? = 0$. $6 \times 0 = 0$. Write the 0 above the 0 in the dividend. Bring down the 1.

$$
\begin{array}{r}
20 \\
6{\overline{\smash{)}\,12012}} \\
\underline{-\ 12} \\
001
\end{array}
$$

$6 \times ? = 1$. $6 \times 1 = 6$. 1 is too large. Use 0. Write the 0 above the 1, multiply, and subtract. Bring down the 2.

$$
\begin{array}{r}
200 \\
6{\overline{\smash{)}\,12012}} \\
\underline{-\ 12} \\
001 \\
\underline{-\ 0} \\
12
\end{array}
$$

$6 \times ? = 12$. $6 \times 2 = 12$. Write the 2 above the 2 in the dividend. Subtract. The *quotient* is 2002.

$$
\begin{array}{r}
2002 \\
6{\overline{\smash{)}\,12012}} \\
\underline{-\ 12} \\
001 \\
\underline{-\ 0} \\
12 \\
\underline{-\ 12} \\
0
\end{array}
$$

Check your answer:

$$
\begin{array}{r}
2002 \\
\times\ \ \ \ 6 \\
\hline
12{,}012
\end{array}
$$

Divide, then check your answer.

1. $8\overline{)40560}$ 6. $9\overline{)2043}$ 11. $5\overline{)13215}$

2. $2\overline{)97148}$ 7. $4\overline{)99916}$ 12. $4\overline{)27340}$

3. $2\overline{)45664}$ 8. $2\overline{)50816}$ 13. $3\overline{)17622}$

4. $9\overline{)51075}$ 9. $5\overline{)1115}$ 14. $8\overline{)51096}$

5. $3\overline{)30012}$ 10. $6\overline{)13830}$ 15. $3\overline{)23523}$

Divide.

16. $6\overline{)588060}$ 22. $9\overline{)221022}$ 28. $9\overline{)181305}$

17. $9\overline{)54036}$ 23. $4\overline{)315452}$ 29. $8\overline{)293584}$

18. $3\overline{)186342}$ 24. $5\overline{)160025}$ 30. $3\overline{)176322}$

19. $7\overline{)161784}$ 25. $6\overline{)540684}$ 31. $4\overline{)315328}$

20. $5\overline{)205680}$ 26. $5\overline{)261435}$ 32. $9\overline{)106092}$

21. $8\overline{)258224}$ 27. $2\overline{)159972}$ 33. $7\overline{)242109}$

7-3   One-Digit Divisors with Remainders

Example: $5\overline{)517}$

Divide 517 by 5.

$$
\begin{array}{r}
103 \\
5\overline{)517} \\
-5 \\
\hline
01 \\
-0 \\
\hline
17 \\
-15 \\
\hline
2
\end{array}
$$

The last digit in the dividend is 7. There are no more digits to bring down. There is a *remainder* of 2. We write this *remainder* as *r.2* next to the quotient.

$$\begin{array}{r} 103 \text{ r. } 2 \\ 5\overline{)517} \\ -5 \\ \hline 01 \\ -0 \\ \hline 17 \\ -15 \\ \hline 2 \end{array}$$

To check your answer with a *remainder*, multiply the quotient without remainder by the divisor. Add the remainder. The result should equal the dividend.

$$\begin{array}{r} 103 \\ \times \quad 5 \\ \hline 515 \\ + \quad 2 \\ \hline 517 \end{array}$$ ← quotient without remainder
← divisor

← remainder
← dividend

Exercise 7-D

Divide and check your answers.

1. $5\overline{)804}$
2. $9\overline{)715}$
3. $3\overline{)244}$
4. $8\overline{)345}$
5. $7\overline{)157}$
6. $6\overline{)785}$

7. $4\overline{)653}$
8. $2\overline{)313}$
9. $5\overline{)107}$
10. $4\overline{)769}$
11. $2\overline{)355}$
12. $8\overline{)887}$

13. $5\overline{)678}$
14. $9\overline{)342}$
15. $7\overline{)261}$
16. $7\overline{)247}$
17. $3\overline{)920}$
18. $4\overline{)999}$

Divide and check your answers.

19. $3\overline{)7241}$
20. $9\overline{)7732}$
21. $9\overline{)97561}$

22. $6\overline{)4296}$
23. $7\overline{)6519}$
24. $4\overline{)1003}$

25. $9\overline{)6352}$
26. $5\overline{)3118}$
27. $8\overline{)2014}$

28. $7\overline{)6517}$ 31. $6\overline{)40827}$ 34. $2\overline{)11113}$

29. $6\overline{)7394}$ 32. $7\overline{)14356}$ 35. $8\overline{)46372}$

30. $9\overline{)8153}$ 33. $9\overline{)90908}$ 36. $3\overline{)93817}$

7-4 Dividing with Two-Digit Divisors

Example: $20\overline{)260}$

$20 \times ? = 26$. $20 \times 1 = 20$. Write the 1 above the 6.
Multiply 1×20 and subtract the product from 26.
Bring down the 0.

$$\begin{array}{r} 1 \\ 20\overline{)260} \\ -20 \\ \hline 60 \end{array}$$

$20 \times ? = 60$. $20 \times 3 = 60$. Write the 3 above the 0.
Multiply 20×3 and subtract the product from 60.

$$\begin{array}{r} 13 \\ 20\overline{)260} \\ -20 \\ \hline 60 \\ -60 \\ \hline 0 \end{array}$$

Check your answer:

$$\begin{array}{r} 13 \quad \leftarrow \text{quotient} \\ \times \ 20 \quad \leftarrow \text{divisor} \\ \hline 00 \\ + \ 26 \\ \hline 260 \quad \leftarrow \text{dividend} \end{array}$$

Example: $12\overline{)4567}$

$12 \times ? = 45$. $12 \times 3 = 36$. $12 \times 4 = 48$. 4 is too large.
3 is correct. Write the 3 above the 5. Multiply and
subtract. Bring down the 6.

$$\begin{array}{r} 3 \\ 12\overline{)4567} \\ -36 \\ \hline 96 \end{array}$$

$12 \times ? = 96$. $12 \times 8 = 96$. Write the 8 above the 6,
multiply, and subtract. Bring down the 7.

$$\begin{array}{r} 38 \\ 12\overline{)4567} \\ -36 \\ \hline 96 \\ - \ 96 \\ \hline 07 \end{array}$$

$12 \times ? = 7$. $12 \times 0 = 0$. $12 \times 1 = 12$. 1 is too large.
0 is correct. Write the 0 above the 7, multiply, and
subtract.

The remainder is 7.

$$
\begin{array}{r}
380 \text{ r.7} \\
12\overline{)\ 4567} \\
-36 \\
\hline
96 \\
-96 \\
\hline
07 \\
-0 \\
\hline
7
\end{array}
$$

Check your answer:

$$
\begin{array}{r}
380 \leftarrow \text{quotient without remainder} \\
\times \quad 12 \leftarrow \text{divisor} \\
\hline
760 \\
+ \ 380 \\
\hline
4560 \\
+ \qquad 7 \leftarrow \text{remainder} \\
\hline
4567 \leftarrow \text{dividend}
\end{array}
$$

Exercise 7-E

Divide, then check your answers.

1. $25\overline{)\,250}$ 7. $15\overline{)\,915}$ 13. $54\overline{)\,756}$

2. $12\overline{)\,432}$ 8. $24\overline{)\,720}$ 14. $25\overline{)\,375}$

3. $15\overline{)\,300}$ 9. $30\overline{)\,900}$ 15. $12\overline{)\,420}$

4. $50\overline{)\,200}$ 10. $10\overline{)\,270}$ 16. $88\overline{)\,528}$

5. $11\overline{)\,143}$ 11. $22\overline{)\,704}$ 17. $16\overline{)\,880}$

6. $21\overline{)\,357}$ 12. $18\overline{)\,648}$ 18. $20\overline{)\,660}$

Divide, then check your answers.

19. $17\overline{)\,2261}$ 23. $60\overline{)\,1860}$ 27. $30\overline{)\,2700}$

20. $12\overline{)\,1056}$ 24. $10\overline{)\,5500}$ 28. $10\overline{)\,4730}$

21. $30\overline{)\,1440}$ 25. $45\overline{)\,1620}$ 29. $99\overline{)\,2475}$

22. $36\overline{)\,1296}$ 26. $35\overline{)\,1225}$ 30. $78\overline{)\,1404}$

31. $55 \overline{)1375}$

32. $75 \overline{)1950}$

33. $16 \overline{)1280}$

34. $20 \overline{)2440}$

35. $25 \overline{)9125}$

36. $11 \overline{)2816}$

<hr>

Exercise 7-F

Divide, then check your answers.

1. $13 \overline{)427}$

2. $52 \overline{)893}$

3. $23 \overline{)371}$

4. $20 \overline{)678}$

5. $25 \overline{)998}$

6. $12 \overline{)834}$

7. $30 \overline{)837}$

8. $21 \overline{)853}$

9. $11 \overline{)840}$

10. $63 \overline{)764}$

11. $13 \overline{)849}$

12. $22 \overline{)845}$

13. $30 \overline{)788}$

14. $15 \overline{)349}$

15. $32 \overline{)849}$

16. $10 \overline{)677}$

17. $25 \overline{)612}$

18. $30 \overline{)891}$

Divide, then check your answers.

19. $15 \overline{)1293}$

20. $25 \overline{)3992}$

21. $12 \overline{)5991}$

22. $31 \overline{)1119}$

23. $71 \overline{)2485}$

24. $30 \overline{)7884}$

25. $62 \overline{)5998}$

26. $70 \overline{)8439}$

27. $68 \overline{)4051}$

28. $22 \overline{)3849}$

29. $19 \overline{)3900}$

30. $15 \overline{)29304}$

31. $20 \overline{)49332}$

32. $11 \overline{)39992}$

33. $65 \overline{)93333}$

34. $25 \overline{)39454}$

35. $12 \overline{)39445}$

36. $50 \overline{)29304}$

<hr>

7-5 Inverse Operations

In Chapter 5, we learned that addition and subtraction are *inverse operations*. Multiplication and division are also *inverse operations*. Each multiplication problem has its *inverse* division problem, and each division problem has its *inverse* multiplication problem.

Multiplication	Inverse Operation (Division)
$3 \times 2 = 6$	$6 \div 2 = 3$ and $6 \div 3 = 2$
$7 \times 3 = 21$	$21 \div 3 = 7$ and $21 \div 7 = 3$

Division	Inverse Operation (Multiplication)
$10 \div 5 = 2$	$2 \times 5 = 10$ or $5 \times 2 = 10$
$12 \div 4 = 3$	$3 \times 4 = 12$ or $4 \times 3 = 12$

We can use *inverse operations* to check answers.

Problem	Check
$36 \times 3 = 108$	$108 \div 3 = 36$ or $108 \div 36 = 3$
$24 \div 6 = 4$	$4 \times 6 = 24$ or $6 \times 4 = 24$

Exercise 7-G

Check each problem by writing two *inverse* division problems.

1. $10 \times 2 = 20$ *$20 \div 2 = 10$ or $20 \div 10 = 2$*
2. $7 \times 4 = 28$
3. $4 \cdot 3 = 12$
4. $6 \cdot 7 = 42$
5. $(9)(8) = 72$
6. $20 \times 3 = 60$
7. $12 \cdot 3 = 36$
8. $1 \cdot 9 = 9$
9. $(8)4 = 32$
10. $11 \times 2 = 22$
11. $12 \times 4 = 48$
12. $25(3) = 75$
13. $24 \cdot 4 = 96$
14. $15 \times 4 = 60$
15. $(9)(7) = 63$
16. $35 \times 2 = 70$
17. $33(4) = 132$
18. $50 \times 5 = 250$
19. $22 \cdot 4 = 88$
20. $18 \times 1 = 18$

Check each problem by writing an *inverse* multiplication problem.

21. $25 \div 5 = 5$
22. $54 \div 6 = 9$
23. $75 \div 3 = 25$
24. $88 \div 4 = 22$
25. $125 \div 5 = 25$
26. $340 \div 10 = 34$
27. $542 \div 2 = 271$
28. $712 \div 89 = 8$
29. $236 \div 59 = 4$
30. $228 \div 12 = 19$

In Chapter 5, we used inverse operations to find missing numbers in addition and subtraction problems. We can do the same for multiplication and division problems:

Example: $6 \times \underline{} = 24$

Use the *inverse operation*:

$24 \div 6 = 4$

Answer: $6 \times 4 = 24$

Example: $\underline{} \div 6 = 5$

Use the *inverse operation*:

$5 \times 6 = 30$

Answer: $30 \div 6 = 5$

Exercise 7-H

Use inverse operations to find each missing number.

1. $10 \times \underline{} = 60$
2. $8 \times \underline{} = 56$
3. $7 \times \underline{} = 49$
4. $25 \times \underline{} = 200$
5. $5 \times \underline{} = 455$
6. $3 \times \underline{} = 201$
7. $\underline{} \times 9 = 2925$
8. $\underline{} \times 8 = 624$
9. $6 \times \underline{} = 750$
10. $6 \times \underline{} = 5304$
11. $4 \times \underline{} = 392$
12. $\underline{} \times 9 = 261$
13. $50 \times \underline{} = 750$
14. $\underline{} \times 20 = 800$
15. $35 \times \underline{} = 1155$
16. $40 \times \underline{} = 400$
17. $\underline{} \times 25 = 1075$
18. $75 \times \underline{} = 6150$

Use inverse operations to find each missing number.

19. $\underline{} \div 7 = 6$
20. $\underline{} \div 8 = 8$
21. $\underline{} \div 12 = 3$
22. $\underline{} \div 10 = 10$
23. $\underline{} \div 8 = 25$
24. $\underline{} \div 4 = 23$
25. $\underline{} \div 7 = 19$
26. $\underline{} \div 12 = 1$
27. $\underline{} \div 15 = 80$
28. $\underline{} \div 19 = 46$
29. $\underline{} \div 16 = 77$
30. $\underline{} \div 9 = 127$

31. ___ ÷ 18 = 455

32. ___ ÷ 8 = 1,250

33. ___ ÷ 22 = 0

34. ___ ÷ 65 = 254

35. ___ ÷ 99 = 99

36. ___ ÷ 128 = 5,499

7-7 Multiples of Ten

In Chapter 6, we learned how to multiply numbers by multiples of ten (multiplying the nonzero digits and combining the numbers of zeros). Now we will learn how to *divide* by multiples of ten.

To divide a multiple of ten by a multiple of ten, we cross out zeros in the divisor and dividend, then divide the numbers.

Example:

$$24,000 \div 100$$

The dividend 24,000 has 3 zeros. The divisor 100 has 2 zeros. Cross out the *lesser* number of zeros in both the divisor and dividend:

Cross out 2 zeros: 24,0∅∅ ÷ 1∅∅

Divide: $240 \div 1 = 240$

Example:

$$120,000 \div 600$$

$\uparrow$ 4 zeros $\uparrow$ 2 zeros

Cross out 2 zeros in both divisor and dividend:

120,0∅∅ ÷ 6∅∅

Divide: $1,200 \div 6 = 200$

Example:

$$1,260 \div 200$$

$\uparrow$ 1 zero $\uparrow$ 2 zeros

Cross out 1 zero from both divisor and dividend. Then divide:

1,26∅ ÷ 20∅

$126 \div 20 = 6 \text{ r. } 6$

Cross out the zeros and divide.

1. $350 \div 70$
2. $36,000 \div 600$
3. $12,000 \div 60$
4. $1,800 \div 90$
5. $2,000 \div 200$
6. $45,000,000 \div 9,000$
7. $11,000 \div 1,000$
8. $1,500,000 \div 3,000$
9. $28,000 \div 700$
10. $4,200,000 \div 60,000$
11. $8,200,000 \div 2,000$
12. $240,000 \div 1,200$
13. $15,600,000 \div 3,000$
14. $56,000, \div 1,400$
15. $3,600 \div 1,800$

16. $90,000,000 \div 30,000$
17. $33,000 \div 1,100$
18. $85,000 \div 5,000$
19. $300 \div 120$
20. $63,500 \div 2,000$
21. $18,750 \div 100$
22. $13,000 \div 70$
23. $15,000 \div 400$
24. $2,300 \div 60$
25. $9,000 \div 800$
26. $12,400 \div 500$
27. $11,000,000 \div 6,000$
28. $6,800 \div 270$
29. $19,000 \div 700$
30. $17,000,000 \div 3000$

7-8 Order of Operations

Example:

$$3 + 2 \times 6$$

Which answer is correct?

$$3 + 2 \times 6 =$$
$$5 \quad \times 6 = 30$$

or

$$3 + 2 \times 6 =$$
$$3 + \quad 12 = 15$$

When we have a problem with *more* than one kind of operation (addition and multiplication, for example) we must follow the **Rules of Order**.

RULES OF ORDER.

1. Always begin at the left side.

2. First, do all multiplication and division, *in order*.
   If multiplication comes *before* division, do the multiplication first.
   If division comes *before* multiplication, do the division first.

3. Next, do all addition and subtraction, *in order.*
   If addition comes *before* subtraction, do the addition first.
   If subtraction comes *before* addition, do the subtraction first.

In the problem above,

$$3 + 2 \times 6 =$$

multiply
↓
$$3 + 2 \times 6 =$$

$$3 + \quad 12 \quad = 15$$
↑
then add

Example:

$$10 \div 5 + 3 + 4 \times 2 - 4$$

Begin at the left side and do all multiplication and division, in order:

divide
↓
$$10 \div 5 + 3 + 4 \times 2 - 4$$

multiply
↓
$$2 + 3 + 4 \times 2 - 4$$

$$2 + 3 + 8 - 4$$

Then do all addition and subtraction, in order:

add
↓
$$2 + 3 + 8 - 4$$

add
↓
$$5 + 8 - 4$$

$$13 - 4 = 9$$

Use the *Rules of Order* to find the answers.

1. $4 \times 4 - 3 \times 5$
2. $10 - 3 + 4 - 1$
3. $9 \times 4 - 30 \div 6$
4. $21 \div 7 + 3$
5. $12 - 4 \times 2$
6. $64 \div 8 \times 2 \div 4$
7. $8 + 4 \div 2 + 5 - 10$
8. $6 \times 5 - 5 \times 4$
9. $10 \div 2 - 3 + 6 \times 5$
10. $36 - 42 \div 7 \times 6$
11. $15 - 10 + 5 - 3$
12. $18 - 8 \div 2 - 4 \div 2$
13. $6 \times 3 - 5 \times 2$
14. $6 + 15 \div 5 - 20 \div 10$
15. $18 \times 2 - 9 \div 3$
16. $25 \div 5 \times 4 + 6 - 2$
17. $24 \div 8 - 2$
18. $12 + 20 \div 4 - 5$
19. $34 - 4 \div 4 + 16 \times 2$
20. $8 \times 8 + 9 \div 3 - 60$

21. $6 + 4 \div 2 \times 7 - 11$
22. $15 \div 3 \times 3 - 15$
23. $6 + 14 - 8 \div 4 - 3 \div 3$
24. $35 - 10 \times 3 + 2 \div 2 + 6$
25. $24 \div 8 + 3 \times 6$
26. $16 \times 2 - 1$
27. $10 \times 2 - 1 \times 5$
28. $12 - 4 \times 2 + 6 \div 3 + 3$
29. $7 \times 7 + 10 \div 2 - 20$
30. $56 \div 7 \times 3 - 5 \times 2$
31. $15 \times 3 - 2 \times 8$
32. $11 - 4 \times 2 + 6 \times 2 - 2$
33. $12 \div 4 \times 2 - 6$
34. $5 + 13 - 8 \div 4 - 4 \div 2 + 3$
35. $8 + 16 - 10 \div 2 - 7 \div 7$
36. $25 - 3 \times 5 + 8 \div 1 + 4 - 3$
37. $20 \div 4 - 5 \div 1$
38. $12 \div 6 + 3 + 2 \times 4 - 4$
39. $16 - 5 + 72 \div 9 + 4 \times 3 - 12$
40. $25 + 6 \div 2 \times 2 + 9 - 4 \div 2$

7-9 More Order of Operations

When there are *parentheses* ( ), brackets [ ], or braces { }, we follow these **Rules of Order.**

RULES OF ORDER:

1. Always begin at the left side.
2. First, do all operations inside the parentheses, brackets, or braces, *in order.*
3. If there are parentheses inside brackets [( )], do the operation in parentheses first, then do the operation in brackets.

$$\text{add first}$$
$$\downarrow$$
$$[4 \times (3 + 5)]$$
$$\uparrow$$
$$\text{then multiply}$$

4. When there are no more parentheses or brackets, follow the *Rules of Order* given in Section 7-8.

Example:

$$17 - (3 + 1) \times 4$$

$$\text{add}$$
$$\downarrow$$
$$17 - (3 + 1) \times 4$$

$$\text{multiply}$$
$$\downarrow$$
$$17 - 4 \times 4$$

$$17 - 16 = 1$$

Example:

$$3 + [3 \times (4 + 2)] \div 6$$

$$\text{add}$$
$$\downarrow$$
$$3 + [3 \times (4 + 2)] \div 6$$

$$\text{multiply}$$
$$\downarrow$$
$$3 + [3 \times 6] \div 6$$

$$\text{divide}$$
$$\downarrow$$
$$3 + 18 \div 6$$

$$3 + 3 = 6$$

Use the *Rules of Order* to find the answers.

1. $6 + (2 - 1)$
2. $7 \times (5 - 3)$
3. $4 \times (5 + 1) - 4 \div 2$
4. $\{9 + (3 + 4)\}$
5. $6 + \{4 - (6 - 4)\}$
6. $15 - (4 + 4)$
7. $8 \div (2 \times 2) \times 9$
8. $80 - [10 \times (3 + 2)]$
9. $6 \times (3 + 5)$
10. $17 + (2 + 4)$
11. $9 + (6 \times 3) \div 6$
12. $2 \times [(4 + 6) - 3]$
13. $65 - (15 + 2)$
14. $(6 - 3) \times (9 - 6)$

15. $6 \times 3 - (2 \times 6 + 3)$
16. $(81 \div 9) \div 3$
17. $(7 - 3) \div (11 - 9)$
18. $7 \times (3 - 2) \times 4 + 3 \times 2$
19. $4 + [(6 \times 2) + 3]$
20. $96 \div (12 \times 4) \div 2$
21. $43 + (24 - 20)$
22. $6 \times 7 - (4 + 9)$
23. $4 \times (42 - 11)$
24. $7 \times [(12 + 5) - 3 \times (19 - 14)]$
25. $6 \times 3 + (4 \times 3 + 2 \times 6)$
26. $7 \times (5 + 28) \div 7$
27. $171 - (17 + 4) \times 2 \times 3 - 30$
28. $3 \times (4 + 5) - 7$

Complete the sentences with the following words:

divisor	inverse	divided by
quotient	factors	product
distributive	commutative	parentheses
multiply	times	multiplicative property of zero

1. Multiplication and division are _____ operations.
2. The _____ of 3 and 2 is 6.
3. $7 \times 3 = 3 \times 7$ is an example of the _____ property.
4. The answer in a division problem is called the _____.
5. We read $\div$ as _____.
6. Seven _____ three equals twenty-one.
7. $4 \times 0 = 0$ is an example of the _____ property.

8. The number we divide by is called the _____.

9. In $7 + 3 \times 2$, we _____ first.

10. The numbers we multiply together are called _____.

11. ( ) are called _____.

12. $8(2 + 6) = 8 \times 2 + 8 \times 6$ is an example of the _____ property.

LET'S TALK ABOUT ...

1. division	5. remainder
2. divisor	6. parentheses
3. quotient	7. brackets
4. dividend	8. order of operations

7-10 Solving Division Word Problems

Example:

*Together, John and Julius earn $324 in 1 week. If they earn equal amounts, how much money does **each** receive?*

The word *each* tells us that this is a division problem. We must divide by 2, because there are two people who receive equal amounts of money.

Answer: $324 \div 2 = \$162$ each

Example:

*Marianne stayed at a hotel for 7 days. The total bill was $511. How much did she pay **per day**?*

The words *per day* mean *for each day*. We divide by 7 to find the cost for *each* day.

Answer: $511 \div 7 = \$73$ per day

Peter works at the **Grand Hotel**. He is manager of the restaurant there. This Saturday night, seniors from Tech High School will go to the Grand Hotel for a special dinner party and dance. Peter needs to prepare the tables.

1. 216 students will eat dinner at the restaurant. Each table can seat nine people. How many tables will Peter need?

2. There will be 36 teachers at the dinner. The teachers will *not* sit with the students. How many tables does Peter need for the teachers only?

3. How many tables will there be altogether?

4. How many people will there be altogether?

5. Peter will divide 12 dozen flowers evenly among the student tables.
   a. How many flowers does he have in all?
   b. How many flowers will he put on each student table?

6. The kitchen has 650 forks in all for the teachers and students. Will each person receive two or three forks?

7. Peter needs to divide the students into four separate groups around the dance floor.
   a. How many student tables will be in each group?
   b. How many students will be in each group?

8. The students and teachers will arrive at 7:00 P.M. and leave at 11:30 P.M.
   a. Will they be there longer than 5 hours?
   b. How many *minutes* will they spend at the Hotel?

9. The students and teachers will eat dinner first, then dance. If they spend *equal* time eating and dancing, how many minutes will the students need to eat?

In solving the word problems in Exercise 7-L, we used the *quotient alone* as the answer. When we have division problems with *remainders*, we sometimes use the *remainder alone*, or we use both the *remainder and the quotient* together for our answer. Study the following example.

Example:

There are 115 students who need to take a math class. Each classroom can seat no more than 30 students.

(a) *How many classrooms will be needed?*

Divide:

$$
\begin{array}{r}
3 \\
30\overline{)115} \\
-90 \\
\hline
25
\end{array}
$$

3 classrooms of 30 students

25 students (remainder) to go to 1 more classroom

Answer: We will need 4 classrooms (3 + 1) to seat 115 students. We use the *quotient* (3) and the *remainder* (25) to get our answer.

(b) *How many classrooms will be full (classrooms with 30 students)?*

$$
\begin{array}{r}
3 \\
30\overline{)115} \\
-90 \\
\hline
25
\end{array}
$$

3 classrooms of 30 students

Answer: 3 classrooms will be full. We use the *quotient only* to get our answer.

(c) *How many classrooms will not be full (will have fewer than 30 students)?*

$$
\begin{array}{r}
3 \\
30\overline{)115} \\
-90 \\
\hline
25
\end{array}
$$

25 students in 1 classroom

Answer: 1 classroom of 25 students. We use the *remainder only* to get our answer.

The Grayson family is planning a family camping trip. There are 34 members in the Grayson family, including uncles, aunts, and cousins. They will go to Silver Lake for one week.

1. The Graysons will travel by car. Each car seats five people. How many cars will they need to take?

2. They will bring tents for sleeping.
   Each tent can sleep up to six people.
   a. How many tents will they need?
   b. How many tents will be *full*?
   c. How many tents will *not* be full?

3. Kevin Grayson will bring 36 poles to hold the tents. How many poles will he use for each tent?

4. The children will hike (walk) around the lake. They will divide into groups of six. There are 21 Grayson children altogether.
   a. How many *full* groups (groups of six) will there be?
   b. How many children will be in a group of fewer than six?
   c. How many groups will they need altogether?

5. Martha Grayson will buy apples for everyone. She will buy 70 apples altogether.
   a. How many apples will each person have to eat?
   b. How many extra apples will there be?

109

6. Betty Grayson will buy drinks for everyone. She estimates that each person will drink 4 cans of sodas. How many cans does she need?

7. The sodas come in 6-packs (6 cans in a pack). How many 6-packs does she need to buy?

8. They will rent boats at the lake. Each boat can hold up to seven people.
   a. How many boats do they need?
   b. How many boats will be *full*?
   c. How many people will be in a boat that has fewer than seven people?

9. Each boat costs $18 a day to rent.
   a. How much will they spend on boat rentals for 1 day?
   b. If they have $300 to spend, how many days can they rent the boats?

Write with *words*.

1. $12 \div 6 = 2$
2. $24 \div 3 = 8$
3. $15 \div 5 = 3$
4. $21 \div 7 = 3$
5. $72 \div 8 = 9$
6. $42 \div 6 = 7$

Complete.

7. $32 \div 8 = 4$ Dividend: ____   Divisor: ____   Quotient: ____

Divide. Rewrite if necessary.

8. $64 \div 8$
9. $63 \div 7$
10. $345 \div 5$
11. $236 \div 4$
12. $5{,}004 \div 6$
13. $796 \div 5$
14. $205 \div 4$
15. $34{,}003 \div 8$
16. $216 \div 12$
17. $1{,}650 \div 25$
18. $7{,}566 \div 20$
19. $60{,}544 \div 90$

Use *inverse operations* to find the missing numbers.

20. $12 \times \underline{\ \ } = 3{,}660$
21. $\underline{\ \ } \div 15 = 23$
22. $\underline{\ \ } + 742 = 3{,}245$
23. $609 + \underline{\ \ } = 1{,}233$
24. $\underline{\ \ } - 34 = 214$
25. $\underline{\ \ } - 717 = 0$

Multiply or divide by combining or crossing out zeros.

26. $2{,}300{,}000 \div 1{,}000$
27. $4{,}500 \times 100$
28. $340 \times 2{,}000{,}000$
29. $16{,}000{,}000 \div 800$
30. $36{,}000 \div 1{,}200$
31. $2{,}500 \times 200 \times 3{,}000$

Use the rules of order to solve.

32. $64 \div 8 \times 2 \div 4$
33. $34 - 4 \div 4 + 16 \times 2$
34. $\{9 \times (3 + 4)\}$
35. $8 \times [(10 + 3) - 3 \times (18 - 16)]$

36. Nine airplanes will fly to Hawaii. 765 people want to go to Hawaii. How many people will each airplane carry?

37. Jerry earned $135 for 5 hours of work. What is his hourly wage (salary per hour)?

38. Luis drove 960 miles from Los Angeles to Santa Cruz. He used 40 gallons of gasoline. How many miles did he drive on 1 gallon of gas?

39. Each cage at the zoo can hold 15 monkeys. There are 130 monkeys to put into cages.
    a. How many cages does the zoo need?
    b. How many monkeys will be in a cage that is *not* full?

Unit 2 Vocabulary Words

1. Addends   The numbers to be added together: In 3 + 2 = 5, 3 and 2 are called *addends*.

2. Addition   Adding numbers together to result in a sum. 3 + 2 = 5 is an *addition* problem.

3. Additive Identity Property   "Adding zero to any number does not change the sum."

4. Associative Property   "We can group three or more numbers in any way and the sum or product does not change."

5. Commutative Property   "The order of adding or multiplying numbers does not change the sum or product."

6. Difference   The answer in a subtraction problem is *difference*.

7. Distributive Property   "For any numbers x, y, z: $x(y + z) = xy + xz$."

8. Divided by   The symbol ÷. It tells us to divide.

9. Dividend   In 8 ÷ 2 = 4, the dividend is 8.

10. Division   Dividing numbers to result in a quotient: 8 ÷ 4 = 2 is a division problem.

11. Divisor   In 8 ÷ 2 = 4, the divisor is 2.

12. Equal   The symbol =, which means *having the same value*.

13. Factor   The numbers to be multiplied together. In 4 × 3 = 12 the factors are 4 and 3.

14. Inverse Operations   Subtraction and addition are *inverse* operations (3 + 4 = 7 and 7 − 4 = 3). Multiplication and division are *inverse* operations (4 × 2 = 8 and 8 ÷ 2 = 4).

15. Minuend   In 5 − 3 = 2, the minuend is 5.

16. Minus   The symbol −. It tells us to subtract.

17. Multiplication   Multiplying numbers together to result in a product. 5 × 3 = 15 is a multiplication problem.

18. Multiplicative Identity Property   "Multiplying any number by 1 does not change the value of the number."

19. Multiplicative Property of Zero   "Multiplying any number by zero makes the product zero."

20. Parentheses   The symbol ( ). Parentheses are used to group numbers together.

21. Plus   The symbol +. It tells us to add.

22. Product   The answer in a multiplication problem is a *product*.

23. Subtraction	Subtracting two numbers to result in a difference. 5 – 4 = 1 is a subtraction problem.
24. Subtrahend	In the problem 6 – 4 = 2, the subtrahend is 4.
25. Sum	The answer in an addition problem is a *sum*.
26. Times	The symbol ×. It tells us to multiply.

UNIT 3

Number Theory

1 2 3 4 5 6 7 8 9 0 π

1 2 3 4 5 6 7 8 9 0 ⌐

1 2 3 4 5 6 7 8 9 0 ∡

1 2 3 4 5 6 7 8 9 0 +

1 2 3 4 5 6 7 8 9 0 √

0 1 2 3 4 5 6 7 8 9 ÷

√ 0 9 8 7 6 5 4 3 2 1

+ 0 9 8 7 6 5 4 3 2 1

∡ 0 9 8 7 6 5 4 3 2 1

⌐ 0 9 8 7 6 5 4 3 2 1

π 0 9 8 7 6 5 4 3 2 1

Integers

8-1 The Number Line

This is a **number line**:

The number line continues to the right and to the left. There is *no end* to the number line.

The numbers on this number line are called **integers**. There are an *infinite* number of integers on a number line. That means there is *no end* to the number of integers. There are *negative* and *positive* integers:

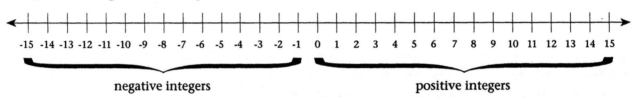

Every positive integer has an opposite negative integer, except 0. A positive integer and its opposite negative integer are called **additive inverses**.

–1 and 1 are additive inverses.
–30 and 30 are additive inverses.

Exercise 8-A

Name the additive inverse of each number.

1. –7
2. 19
3. –33

4. –45
5. 100
6. 98

7. –67
8. 1,344
9. –876

DEFINITION: Whole Numbers

The *positive* integers (0, 1, 2, 3 . . .) are also called **whole numbers**.

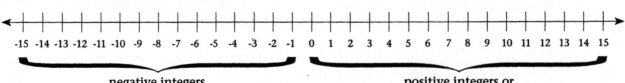

DEFINITION: Even and Odd Integers

Even integers are integers that are *evenly divisible* by 2: 0, 2, 4, 6, 8, . . . except 0. When we divide an even integer by 2, there is *no* remainder.

Odd integers are integers that are *not* evenly divisible by 2: 1, 3, 5, 7, . . . When we divide an odd integer by 2, there *is* a remainder.

Even and odd integers can also be negative:

Even, negative integers: –2, –4, –6, –8, . . .

Odd, negative integers: –1, –3, –5, –7, . . .

Exercise 8-B

Write *even* or *odd* next to each integer.

1. 16 *even*	5. 11	9. 1,151
2. 3	6. 123	10. 2,300
3. –4	7. –200	11. –1,000
4. 0	8. 1,609	12. 2,001

Answer the following questions with integers.

13. What is the odd integer between 10 and 12? *11*

14. What is the even integer between –1 and 2?

15. What is your address *number?*

16. Is your address number an even or odd number?

17. What is the next even integer after 98?

18. What is the next odd integer after 637?

19. How old are you?

20. Is your age an even or odd number?

21. How many odd integers are there between 36 and 49?

22. How many even integers are there between –1 and 15?

23. What is the even integer just before 1,501?

24. Name all the negative even integers between –5 and –19.

25. Name all the negative odd integers between –33 and –52.

8-2 Comparing Integers

On the number line, the integers on the right are *greater than* the integers on the left:

> 3 is greater than 1
> 1 is greater than –3
> –1 is greater than –2

The integers on the left are *less than* the integers on the right:

> 2 is less than 4
> 0 is less than 1
> –4 is less than –3

The symbol for *greater than* is >:

$$4 > 2$$
$$-6 > -12$$

The symbol for *less than* is <:

$$7 < 9$$
$$-1 < 2$$

The symbol for *equal to* is =:

$$3 = 3$$
$$-5 = -5$$

Exercise 8-C

Say the following aloud.

1. $14 < 20$ *"fourteen is less than twenty"*
2. $6 < 14$
3. $19 < 25$
4. $0 = 0$
5. $-2 < 1$
6. $0 > -3$
7. $-16 < -11$
8. $45 > 44$
9. $150 > 50$
10. $-5 < -2$

Use the symbols <, >, or = for each.

11. $164 \leq 641$
12. $150 \_\_ 105$
13. $0 \_\_ -5$
14. $-15 \_\_ -12$
15. $29 \_\_ 29$
16. $-94 \_\_ -95$
17. $675 \_\_ 657$
18. $-410 \_\_ 401$
19. $-2 \_\_ 0$
20. $15 \_\_ 15$
21. $-11 \_\_ -30$
22. $0 \_\_ -6$

Answer the questions with positive or negative integers.

23. Name two odd integers greater than 95. *97 and 99*

24. Name two even integers greater than 27.

25. Name three even, positive integers less than 6.
26. Name two odd, negative integers greater than –5.
27. Name two even, negative integers less than –15.
28. Name two even integers greater than 26 and less than 31.
29. Name three odd integers greater than 0 and less than 7.
30. Name two even negative integers greater than –10 and less than –5.
31. Name two odd negative integers greater than –20 and less than –16.
32. Name an even integer less than 2 and greater than –2.

Write in integers.

33. _15_ < _21_
34. ___ > ___
36. –___ < –___
37. –___ > –___
38. ___ < ___
39. ___ > ___

40. 0 > ___
41. ___ > –___
42. –___ < ___
43. –___ = –___
44. –___ < –___
45. –___ < 0

Exercise 8-D

Write the integers in order, from smallest to greatest.

1. 7, 0, 4, –1
   _–1, 0, 4, 7_
2. 9, –3, –2, 6
3. 3, –8, –2, –7
4. –3, –6, 5, –4
5. 9, 14, –5, –9
6. –6, 6, 3, –3

7. –7, 5, –2, 0
8. –4, –2, 6, 1
9. 14, –7, –5, 5
10. –9, –8, –10, –12
11. 6, 9, –6, –9
12. 6, –7, 4, –8
13. –4, –7, 0, 1

14. –4, –6, –3, –10
15. –3, –5, 3, 5
16. 12, –8, –3, 6
17. 19, –24, –18, 23
18. 0, –1, –3, 4
19. –15, –19, –13, –10
20. 14, 12, 0, –14

LET'S TALK ABOUT ...

1. number line
2. integer
3. positive
4. negative

5. additive inverse
6. whole number
7. even
8. odd

9. greater than
10. less than
11. equal to
12. infinite

What are the additive inverses of the following numbers?

1. 15
2. −3
3. 100
4. 35
5. −156
6. −2,388

Write *odd* or *even* next to each number.

7. 35
8. 10
9. 0
10. 1,800
11. 333
12. 2,787

Write with *words*.

13. 4 > 2
14. 9 < 18
15. −4 > −15
16. −9 < 0
17. 25 = 25
18. 6 > −3

Use the symbols <, >, or =.

19. 37 ___ 45
20. −15 ___ 0
21. 9 ___ 19
22. 0 ___ −12
23. −24 ___ −55
24. 950 ___ 905
25. −55 ___ 55
26. −222 ___ −222
27. 98 ___ −98

Write the integers in order, from smallest to greatest.

28. 12, 6, 0 7
29. −4, 7, −5, 10
30. 34, 43, −13, −4
31. −19, 0, −45, −8
32. 456, 355, 534, 435
33. −45, −66, −13, −54
34. 8, − 7, 0, −9
35. −11, −10, −12, −9
36. 34, 43, 54, 45

9 Prime Numbers, Bases, and Exponents

9-1 Prime Numbers

In Chapter 6 we studied *factors*. Factors are the numbers we multiply together to result in a product.

Example:

What are the factors of 8?

$$8 = 1 \times 8$$
$$8 = 2 \times 4$$

The factors of 8 are 1, 8, 2, and 4. There are four factors of 8.

Some numbers have only two factors. Other numbers have more than two factors:

$$7 = 1 \times 7$$
$$12 = 1 \times 12$$
$$= 2 \times 6$$
$$= 3 \times 4$$

The number 7 has only two factors. The number 12 has six factors.

Exercise 9-A

Name all the factors for each number and state how many factors there are.

	Factors	How many?		Factors	How many?
1. 14	$1 \times 14, 2 \times 7$	4	11. 24		
2. 40			12. 35		
3. 48			13. 100		
4. 11			14. 23		
5. 28			15. 56		
6. 36			16. 13		
7. 5			17. 99		
8. 12			18. 33		
9. 19			19. 150		
10. 27			20. 80		

DEFINITION: Prime Number

A **prime number** is a number greater than 1 that has *exactly* two factors. The factors are: 1 and the number itself.

The following are examples of some prime numbers and their factors:

$$2 = 1 \times 2 \qquad\qquad 7 = 1 \times 7$$
$$3 = 1 \times 3 \qquad\qquad 11 = 1 \times 11$$
$$5 = 1 \times 5 \qquad\qquad 13 = 1 \times 13$$

Because there are an infinite number of integers, there are also an *infinite* number of prime numbers.

DEFINITION: Composite Number

A **composite number** is a number greater than 1 that is *not* prime. All composite numbers have *more* than two factors.

Examples of *composite numbers*: 4, 6, 8, 9

Their factors are:
$$4 = 1 \times 4 \qquad 6 = 1 \times 6 \qquad 8 = 1 \times 8 \qquad 9 = 1 \times 9$$
$$= 2 \times 2 \qquad\quad = 2 \times 3 \qquad\quad = 2 \times 4 \qquad\quad = 3 \times 3$$

There are an *infinite* number of composite numbers.

The number 1 has only one factor, but it is *not* a prime number. A prime number is a number greater than one. It is *not* a composite number, either because it has only one factor.

Exercise 9-B

Write *prime* or *composite* next to each number.

1. 10 composite	7. 21	13. 9
2. 11	8. 17	14. 5
3. 15	9. 22	15. 23
4. 2	10. 29	16. 45
5. 33	11. 39	17. 19
6. 27	12. 3	18. 100

Answer the following.

19. Name all the prime numbers between 1 and 20.

20. What is a prime number greater than 30 and less than 35?

21. How many prime numbers are there between 10 and 20?

22. Name the prime numbers between 10 and 20.

23. What is the smallest prime number?

24. How many prime numbers are there altogether?

25. Name all the composite numbers between 1 and 30.

9-2 | Prime Factors

When the factors of a number are *prime numbers*, they are called **prime factors**. Examples of prime factors:

$$6 = 3 \times 2$$
$$35 = 5 \times 7$$
$$21 = 7 \times 3$$

Since all the factors above are *prime numbers*, we call them *prime factors*.

$$24 = 4 \times 6$$
$$16 = 2 \times 8$$
$$20 = 2 \times 10$$

In the examples above, the factors 4, 6, 8, and 10 are *not* prime numbers, so they are *not* prime factors of 24, 16, and 20.

We can write prime factors for composite numbers (24, 16, 20):

$$24 = 2 \times 2 \times 2 \times 3$$
$$16 = 2 \times 2 \times 2 \times 2$$
$$20 = 2 \times 2 \times 5$$

but we *cannot* write prime factors for *prime numbers:*

$$2 = 1 \times 2 \qquad\qquad 5 = 1 \times 5$$
$$7 = 1 \times 7 \qquad\qquad 13 = 1 \times 13$$
$$11 = 1 \times 11 \qquad\qquad 17 = 1 \times 17$$
$$\uparrow \qquad\qquad\qquad \uparrow$$

1 is *not* a prime number

Since 1 is a factor for every prime number, and 1 is *not* a prime number, we cannot write prime factors for prime numbers.

Exercise 9-C

Write two factors for each number. Use prime factors.

1. 15 *3 × 5*	5. 25	9. 35
2. 22	6. 9	10. 26
3. 21	7. 14	11. 33
4. 6	8. 55	12. 65

There is an easy way to find the prime factors of a composite number. We use **factor trees**. The lines / \ are called the *branches* of the tree.

Example:

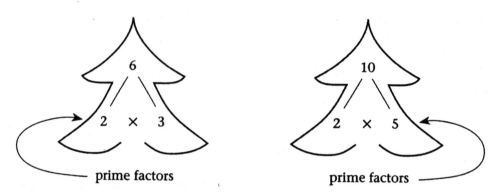

prime factors   prime factors

To make a *factor tree*:

1. For every composite number, write two factors. Draw two branches between the number and factors:

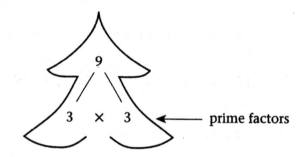

prime factors

2. If any factor is composite, write two more factors, with branches. *Bring down* any prime factor.

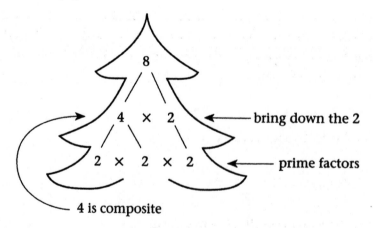

bring down the 2

prime factors

4 is composite

3. When all the numbers on the last line are *prime*, you have found the *prime factors* of that number.

Draw factor trees for each number and find the prime factors.

1. 20	7. 39	13. 63	19. 64
2. 25	8. 22	14. 96	20. 45
3. 30	9. 100	15. 75	21. 80
4. 36	10. 35	16. 55	22. 90
5. 60	11. 50	17. 56	23. 200
6. 24	12. 16	18. 28	24. 150

9-3 Bases and Exponents

Example:

The prime factors of 8 are 2 × 2 × 2. We can write 2 × 2 × 2 in a shorter form:

use 2 as a factor → 2^3 ← how many factors of 2

Example:

The prime factors of 9 are 3 × 3. Write in a shorter form:

use 3 as a factor → $3 \times 3 = 3^2$ ← how many factors of 3

In 3^2, the number 3 is called the *base*, and the number 2 is called the *exponent*. The *base* tells us the factor. The *exponent* tells us how many factors are multiplied together:

$$3^4 = 3 \times 3 \times 3 \times 3 \qquad 4^2 = 4 \times 4$$
$$6^3 = 6 \times 6 \times 6 \qquad 5^1 = 5$$

We read bases and exponents as:

2^0 = "two to the *zero* power"

2^1 = "two to the *first* power"

2^2 = "two to the *second* power" or "two squared"

2^3 = "two to the *third* power" or "two cubed"

2^4 = "two to the *fourth* power"

We read the base as a *cardinal* number, and we read the exponent as an *ordinal* number.

Read aloud or write with words.

1. 4^3

2. 3^5

3. 9^2

4. 7^1

5. 8^5

6. 6^2

7. 3^0

8. 10^3

9. 9^7

10. 10^2

11. 2^{10}

12. 4^8

Use bases and exponents.

13. $7 \cdot 7 \cdot 7 = 7^3$

14. $5 \cdot 5 \cdot 5$

15. $4 \cdot 4$

16. 9

17. $3 \cdot 3 \cdot 3 \cdot 3$

18. $x \cdot x \cdot x$

19. $2 \cdot 2 \cdot 2 \cdot 2 \cdot 2$

20. 10×10

21. $m \cdot m \cdot m \cdot m$

22. 15

23. $c \cdot c + k \cdot k$

24. $y \cdot y \cdot y \cdot y \cdot y \cdot y$

25. $4 \cdot 4 \cdot 4 \cdot 4 \cdot 4 \cdot 4 \cdot 4 \cdot 4$

26. six squared

27. nine to the seventh power

28. twelve cubed

29. sixteen to the third power

30. y to the eleventh power

31. n cubed

32. a to the b power

33. $m \cdot m \cdot m + n \cdot n \cdot n \cdot n \cdot n$

34. r to the s power

35. x squared

36. $20 \cdot 20 \cdot 20 \cdot 20 \cdot 20 \cdot 20$

37. five cubed

38. two to the eighth power

39. x cubed plus y squared

40. four to the zero power

Multiply and find the answer.

1. $7^3 = 7 \times 7 \times 7 = 343$

2. 3^5

3. 19^2

4. 6^4

5. 13^3

6. 1^8

7. 10^3

8. 12^2

9. 4^3

10. 10^8

11. 8^4

12. 3^4

13. 6^5

14. 2^8

15. 9^4

16. 5^4

17. 36^2

18. 5^5

19. 100^3	23. 1^5	27. 2^9
20. 30^4	24. 25^3	28. 10^1
21. 3^3	25. 50^3	29. 20^3
22. 4^5	26. 9^2	30. 15^3

9-4 Using Base Ten

In Chapter 6 we learned how to multiply quickly by multiples of tens. We added the number of zeros:

$$1,000 \times 100 = 100,000$$

3 zeros + 2 zeros = 5 zeros

Now we can use *exponents* when we multiply by multiples of ten:

$$1,000 \times 100 = 100,000 = 10^5 \leftarrow \text{tells how many zeros}$$

$$1,000 \times 100,000 = 10^8$$

3 zeros + 5 zeros = 8 zeros

When the base is ten, the exponent tells us the number of zeros.

Exercise 9-G

Write the answers in base ten and an exponent.

1. $10 \times 10 = 10^2$
2. 100×10
3. $1,000 \times 1,000$
4. $100 \times 1,000$
5. $100 \times 10,000$
6. $100 \times 100 \times 100$
7. $1,000 \times 10$
8. $100,000,000 \times 10$
9. $100 \times 10 \times 1,000$
10. $100 \times 1,000 \times 10$
11. $100,000$
12. $1,000,000,000$
13. 10
14. $100 \times 1,000 \times 100,000$
15. $1,000,000,000,000,000$

9-5 The Zero Exponent

The zero exponent is a special exponent. It makes all numbers *equal to 1*:

$$3^0 = 1 \qquad 5^0 = 1 \qquad x^0 = 1$$
$$10^0 = 1 \qquad 1^0 = 1 \qquad m^0 = 1$$

Example:

Solve:
$$4^2 + 4^0 =$$
$$\underbrace{4 \times 4} + 1 =$$
$$16 + 1 = 17$$

Exercise 9-H

Solve the following.

1. $5^0 + 5^1 = 1 + 5 = 6$
2. $2^0 + 2^2$
3. 4^0
4. 10^5
5. $3^3 - 3^1$
6. 2^4
7. $9^0 - 2^0$
8. $8^2 + 8^0$

9. 5^3
10. $10^3 + 2^0$
11. $5^2 + 5^2$
12. 20^0
13. $10^4 + 10^0$
14. $9^2 + 7^2 + 10^2$
15. $2^4 + 2^3 + 2^0$
16. $10^4 + 10^2 + 10^1 + 10^0$

17. $20^2 + 3^2$
18. $8^2 + 4^3 + 10^2$
19. $10^3 + 2^3 + 5^0$
20. $8^0 + 17^0 + 4^0$
21. $10^6 + 10^0$
22. $3^4 + 3^1$
23. $2^0 + 1^0 + 2^1$
24. $x^0 - y^0$

LISTEN!

Your teacher will say numbers aloud. Listen. Then on your own paper, write the letter that appears next to the number you hear.

1. a. 40^2
   b. 4^2
   c. 4^1
2. a. $70 > 30$
   b. $17 > 32$
   c. $17 < 32$
3. a. $16 < 12$
   b. $16 > 12$
   c. $12 > 16$
4. a. 5^{30}
   b. 5×30
   c. $5 + 30$
5. a. $11 = m$
   b. $11 \times m$
   c. $11 + m$
6. a. $t - 14$
   b. $14 > t$
   c. $14 < t$

7. a. $x^3 + y^2$
   b. $x^2 + y^2$
   c. $x^2 + y^3$
8. a. $8^2 + 3^2$
   b. $8^3 + 3^3$
   c. $8^2 + 2^3$
9. a. $s\overline{)r}$
   b. $r\overline{)s}$
   c. $s \div r$
10. a. 3×3
    b. 3^2
    c. 2^3
11. a. $10^5 - 100$
    b. $10^5 - 10^2$
    c. $10^5 - 100^2$
12. a. $b \times 4$
    b. b^4
    c. 4^b

13. a. $-6 < -9$
    b. $-6 > -9$
    c. $-6 > 9$
14. a. $m^2 > m^3$
    b. $m^3 < m^2$
    c. $m^3 > m^2$
15. a. $-40 < -14$
    b. $-14 < -40$
    c. $-40 > -14$
16. a. 6^0
    b. 0^6
    c. 6^6
17. a. $4^3 = 81$
    b. $3^4 = 81$
    c. $3^4 = 18$
18. a. 10^{60}
    b. 10^6
    c. 10^{16}

Complete each sentence by choosing *a*, *b*, or *c*.

1. In 10^2, the exponent is:
   a. 10
   b. 2
   c. 3

2. Zero is:
   a. not positive or negative
   b. a negative integer
   c. a positive integer

3. The additive inverse of –3 is:
   a. 3
   b. –3
   c. 0

4. Whole numbers are:
   a. negative and positive integers
   b. negative integers
   c. positive integers

5. 14 is:
   a. an odd integer
   b. an even integer
   c. a negative integer

6. A prime number has:
   a. one factor
   b. two factors
   c. more than two factors

7. 1 is:
   a. a prime number
   b. a composite number
   c. not prime or composite

8. 20 is a:
   a. composite and even integer
   b. composite and odd integer
   c. prime and even integer

9. We say or read exponents as:
   a. cardinal numbers
   b. ordinal numbers
   c. round numbers

10. A number with a zero exponent is:
    a. equal to zero
    b. equal to the number
    c. equal to one

9-6 Expanded Notation

We can write 52 in **expanded notation** as

$$52 = (5 \times 10) + (2 \times 1)$$

There are 5 tens and 2 ones in the number 52.

Example:

*Write 427 in **expanded notation**.*

$$427 = (4 \times 100) + (2 \times 10) + (7 \times 1)$$

Write the following in *expanded notation.*

1. $12 = (1 \times 10) + (2 \times 1)$
2. 26
3. 7
4. 68
5. 219
6. 306
7. 999
8. 2,121
9. 3,456
10. 12,904
11. 125,840
12. 230,090

We can use *base ten* with *exponents* to write numbers in *expanded notation.*

$$3,521 = (3 \times 10^3) + (5 \times 10^2) + (2 \times 10^1) + (1 \times 10^0)$$
$$206 = (2 \times 10^2) + (0 \times 10^1) + (6 \times 10^0)$$

Exercise 9-K

Write in expanded notation, using base ten with exponents.

1. $90 = (9 \times 10^1) + (0 \times 10^0)$
2. 29
3. 10
4. 1
5. 980
6. 600
7. 704
8. 4,001
9. 5,387
10. 1,600
11. 60,525
12. 12,401
13. 75,300
14. 190,026
15. 143,974
16. 2,366,747
17. 23,574,077
18. 254,664,922

Exercise 9-L

Complete the sentences with the following words.

factor	exponent	greater than	two
between	even	beginning	equal
negative	infinite	less than	end
left	integer	one	odd
additive inverse	positive	power	whole numbers

1. A number line has no _____ and no _____.
2. We read x^3 as "x cubed" or "x to the third _____."
3. 0 is a _____ integer.

4. A _____ integer is less than zero.

5. There are an _____ number of integers on the number line.

6. –27 is the _____ _____ of 27.

7. An _____ integer can be divided by 2.

8. To write $m \times m$ with an exponent, we use _____ as the exponent.

9. –7 is a negative, _____ integer.

10. –4 is _____ _____ –3.

11. –2 is _____ –3 and –1.

12. When two integers have the same value, they are _____.

13. A number with a zero exponent is always equal to _____.

14. 6 is less than 7 because 6 is to the _____ of 7 on the number line.

15. In "five cubed," the _____ is 3.

16. 16 is an example of a positive _____.

17. 2 is a _____ of 8.

18. 1 is _____ _____ 0.

19. Positive integers are also called _____ _____.

LET'S TALK ABOUT ...

1. prime number
2. composite number
3. prime factor
4. factor tree
5. exponent
6. base
7. expanded notation

Write *prime* or *composite* next to each integer.

1. 9	5. 21	9. 25
2. 2	6. 200	10. 33
3. 15	7. 13	11. 19
4. 11	8. 3	12 99

Using *factor trees*, write the *prime factors* for each.

13. 45	15. 100	17. 50
14 24	16. 33	18. 18

Write with *words*.

19. 3^2	21. 2^4	23. 100^1
20. 10^3	22. 9^6	24. 8^5

Use bases and exponents.

25. $3 \times 3 \times 3 \times 3$

26. $10 \cdot 10 \cdot 10 \cdot 10 \cdot 10$

27. 7

28. $5 \times 5 \times 5$

29. $m \cdot m \cdot m \cdot m \cdot m \cdot m \cdot m \cdot m$

30. $a \cdot a + b \cdot b \cdot b$

31. twenty cubed

32. nine squared

33. $4 \cdot 4 \cdot 4 \cdot 4 + 2 \cdot 2$

34. 1

35. 13

36. $2 \cdot 2 \cdot 2 \cdot 2 \cdot 2 \cdot 2 \cdot 2 \cdot 2 \cdot 2$

37. *t* to the *y* power

38. six to the first power

39. *r* squared plus *b* cubed

Solve.

40. 7^2	43. 19^0	46. $4^2 + 4^1$
41. 10^5	44. $3^5 + 3^2$	47. $2^3 + 2^2 + 2^0$
42. 2^4	45. $10^3 - 10^2$	48. $9^2 + 9^1 - 9^0$

Unit 3 Vocabulary Words

1. Additive Inverse   A positive integer with its opposite negative integer.

2. Base   In 10^3, the base is 10.

3. Composite Numbers   Numbers greater than 1 that have more than two factors.

4. Even Integers   Integers divisible by 2 (without a remainder), including 0.

5. Expanded Notation   In expanded notation, 327 is: $(3 \times 10^2) + (2 \times 10^1) + (7 \times 10^0)$.

6. Exponent   In 10^3, the exponent is 3.

7. Greater Than   The symbol >. Three is *greater than* 1: $3 > 1$

8. Infinite   Without end.

9. Integer   The numbers . . ., –3, –2, –1, 0, 1, 2, 3, . . .

10. Less Than   The symbol <. One is *less than* three: $1 < 3$

11. Negative Integers   Integers less than 0.

12. Odd Integers   Integers not evenly divisible by 2.

13. Positive Integers   Integers 0 and greater.

14. Prime Factors   Factors that are prime numbers. In $2 \times 3 = 6$, 2 and 3 are prime factors of 6.

15. Prime Number   A number greater than 1 that has exactly two factors: 1 and itself.

16. Whole Numbers   The positive integers 0, 1, 2, 3, ...

UNIT 4

<u>Operations with</u> <u>Decimal Numbers</u>

1 2 3 4 5 6 7 8 9 0 π

1 2 3 4 5 6 7 8 9 0 ⌐

1 2 3 4 5 6 7 8 9 0 ⟋

1 2 3 4 5 6 7 8 9 0 +

1 2 3 4 5 6 7 8 9 0 √

0 1 2 3 4 5 6 7 8 9 ÷

√ 0 9 8 7 6 5 4 3 2 1

+ 0 9 8 7 6 5 4 3 2 1

⟋ 0 9 8 7 6 5 4 3 2 1

⌐ 0 9 8 7 6 5 4 3 2 1

π 0 9 8 7 6 5 4 3 2 1

10-1   Tenths

Look at the integers on the following number line below.

We do not see divisions between 0 and 1, 1 and 2, 2 and 3, and so on, but we *can* make an infinite number of divisions, or points between each integer:

these points are
all less than 1

Let's make 10 equal divisions between 0 and 1:

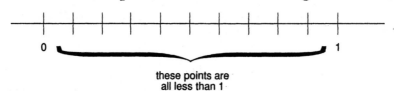

In the number line above, each division, or point, is called a *tenth*:

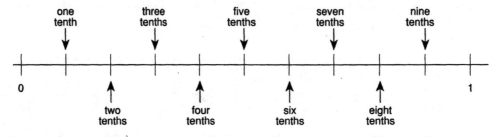

We call these numbers **decimal numbers**, or **decimals**.

We say or write:	As a decimal, we write:	We can also say:
one tenth	.1	"point one"
two tenths	.2	"point two"
three tenths	.3	"point three"
four tenths	.4	"point four"
five tenths	.5	"point five"
six tenths	.6	"point six"
seven tenths	.7	"point seven"
eight tenths	.8	"point eight"
nine tenths	.9	"point nine"

To write a number as **tenths**, we write the number to the right of the decimal point, in the **tenths' place**:

$$\dot{\overline{}}$$
$$\uparrow \quad \uparrow$$
decimal point   tenths' place

Look at the following number line.

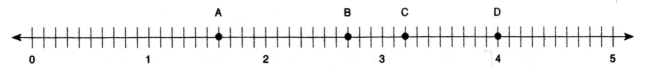

Point *A* = 1.6   We say "one *and* six tenths" or "one point six."

We always read the decimal point as "*and*."

Point *B* = 2.7   We say "two and seven tenths" or "two point seven."
Point *C* = 3.2   We say "three and two tenths" or "three point two."
Point *D* = 4.0   We say "four" or "four point zero."

Exercise 10-A

Identify the points on the number line in three ways.

1. Point *A*   = .2, *two tenths, point two*   4. Point *D*
2. Point *B*   5. Point *E*
3. Point *C*   6. Point *F*

Write with *words*, or say aloud.

7. .5	13. 9.9	19. 20.2
8. .3	14. 2.8	20. 13.3
9. .9	15. 5.4	21. 37.6
10. .2	16. 1.3	22. 11.3
11. .8	17. 12.6	23. 19.4
12. 3.5	18. 14.1	24. 60.5

Write as *decimals*.

25. six tenths = .6   30. six point zero
26. nine tenths   31. fifty and four tenths
27. seven and eight tenths   32. nine point one
28. eight point seven   33. sixty and two tenths
29. three and three tenths   34. three point zero

Compare the decimals. Use < or >.

35. .8 ___ .7
36. .2 ___ .5
37. 6.3 ___ 6.1
38. 5.3 ___ 5.9

39. 7.4 ___ 7.0
40. 6.9 ___ 6.7
41. .9 < 1.0
42. 11.4 ___ 1.4

43. 13.6 ___ 16.3
44. 24.9 ___ 25.0
45. 6.1 ___ 5.9
46. 10.9 ___ 9.1

10-2 Hundredths

Let's make 100 equal divisions between 0 and 1:

0   1

In the number line above, each division, or point, is called a *hundredth*:

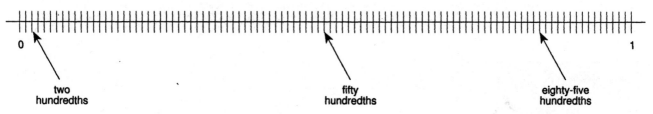

0   1

two
hundredths

fifty
hundredths

eighty-five
hundredths

We say or write:	As a decimal, we write:	We can also say:
one hundredth	.01	"point zero one"
two hundredths	.02	"point zero two"
⋮		⋮
twelve hundredths	.12	"point one two"
⋮		⋮
twenty hundredths	.20	"point two zero"
twenty-one hundredths	.21	"point two one"
⋮		⋮
sixty-four hundredths	.64	"point six four"
⋮		⋮
ninety-eight hundredths	.98	"point nine eight"
ninety-nine hundredths	.99	"point nine nine"

For decimals *greater* than 1:

1   2

1.32

one and thirty-two *hundredths*

We always read the decimal point as *"and"* and we always read the *place name* at the end.

138

To write a number as *hundredths*, we write the last digit of the number to the right of the decimal point in the *hundredths' place*:

$$\overset{\uparrow}{\underset{\text{decimal point}}{}} \quad \overset{\uparrow}{\underset{\text{hundredths' place}}{}}$$

Exercise 10-B

Write with *words*, or say aloud.

1. .09 = *nine hundredths*
2. .11
3. .06
4. .23
5. .19
6. .90

7. 3.40
8. 9.01
9. 16.10
10. 8.22
11. .95
12. 1.00

13. 45.05
14. 18.80
15. 9.91
16. 102.02
17. 13.33
18. 200.02

Write as *decimals*.

19. seven hundredths = *.07*
20. four hundredths
21. thirteen hundredths
22. ten hundredths
23. ninety hundredths
24. point zero one
25. five and three hundredths
26. two point one one
27. nineteen and eleven hundredths
28. seven point zero one

29. twelve point seven two
30. thirteen and nineteen hundredths
31. fifty-five point three six
32. ten and ten hundredths
33. eighteen and one hundredth
34. seven point zero zero
35. thirty and two hundredths
36. ninety-five point six two
37. forty-three and four hundredths
38. one hundred and one hundredth

10-3 Equivalent Decimals in Tenths and Hundredths

Compare .3 with .30

$$\underset{\text{three tenths}}{\overset{\uparrow}{}} \qquad \underset{\text{thirty hundredths}}{\overset{\uparrow}{}}$$

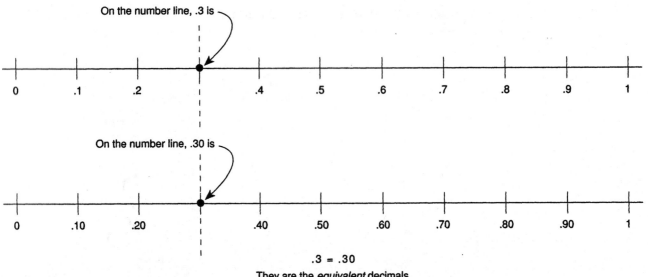

On the number line, .3 is

0   .1   .2   .4   .5   .6   .7   .8   .9   1

On the number line, .30 is

0   .10   .20   .40   .50   .60   .70   .80   .90   1

.3 = .30
They are the *equivalent* decimals.

To change a decimal in *tenths* to an equivalent decimal in *hundredths*, write a zero in the *hundredths'* place:

tenths	→	hundredths	
.2	→	.2<u>0</u>	(.2 = .20)
1.6	→	1.6<u>0</u>	(1.6 = 1.60)

Exercise 10-C

Change the decimals in tenths to equivalent decimals in hundredths.

1. .9 = *.90*
2. .7
3. 6.2
4. 19.0
5. .1

6. 11.3
7. .2
8. 12.4
9. 100.1
10. 23.0

11. 55.5
12. 73.7
13. 256.1
14. 48.8
15. 100.9

10-4   Comparing Decimals in Tenths and Hundredths

Example:

Compare   .6 with .67.
            ↑   ↑
    six tenths   sixty-seven hundredths

To compare decimals in *tenths* and *hundredths*:

1. Change the decimal in tenths to *hundredths*:

.6   .67
↓
.60   .67

2. Now both decimals are in *hundredths*. Compare:

.60 < .67
     so
.6   < .67

Example:

Compare 1.2 with 1.20.

1. Change 1.2 to *hundredths*:

1.2   1.20
↓
1.20   1.20

2. Compare:

1.20 = 1.20
     so
1.2   = 1.20

Exercise 10-D

Compare the decimals. Use <, >, or =.

1. .7 ___ .76
2. .3 ___ .31
3. 1.0 ___ 1.2
4. 9.47 ___ 9.3
5. 6.9 ___ 6.87

6. 4.01 ___ 4.1
7. 17.0 ___ 17.00
8. 11.00 ___ 11.2
9. .4 ___ .43
10. .29 ___ .3

11. .1 ___ .10
12. 72.9 ___ 72.91
13. 9.6 ___ 9.59
14. 6.2 ___ 6.21
15. 21.32 ___ 21.3

10-5   Thousandths

Look at the following number line.

0   1

1,000 divisions

If there are 1,000 divisions between 0 and 1, each point is called a *thousandth*:

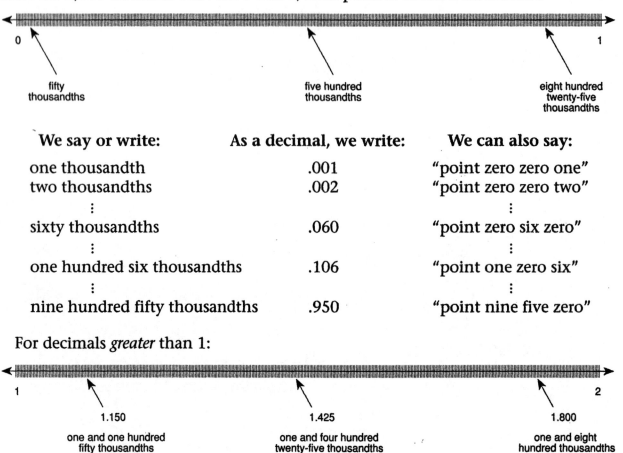

We say or write:	As a decimal, we write:	We can also say:
one thousandth	.001	"point zero zero one"
two thousandths	.002	"point zero zero two"
⋮		⋮
sixty thousandths	.060	"point zero six zero"
⋮		⋮
one hundred six thousandths	.106	"point one zero six"
⋮		⋮
nine hundred fifty thousandths	.950	"point nine five zero"

For decimals *greater* than 1:

To write a number as *thousandths* we write the last digit in the *thousandths' place*, on the right side of the decimal point:

```
. _ _ _
↑ ↑ ↑
│ │ thousandths' place
│ hundredths' place
tenths' place
```

Exercise 10-E

Write with *words*, or say aloud.

1. .003 = *three thousandths*
2. .010
3. .025
4. .102
5. .599
6. .673

7. 2.072
8. 1.002
9. 32.006
10. 13.020
11. 21.200
12. 64.350

13. 173.001
14. 214.035
15. 1.999
16. 17.090
17. 81.003
18. 9.009

Write as *decimals*.

19. seventeen thousandths
20. three thousandths
21. point zero six four
22. four and nineteen thousandths
23. six
24. one point zero one four
25. ninety thousandths
26. fourteen thousandths
27. fifty two and thirty thousandths

28. six hundred eleven thousandths
29. four seven point zero zero nine
30. sixty seven thousandths
31. eight and eighty thousandths
32. ten thousandths
33. three hundred six thousandths
34. eighty-nine thousandths
35. four thousand one and one thousandth

LISTEN!

Your teacher will say decimals aloud. Listen. Then on your own paper, write the letter that appears next to the decimal you hear.

1. a. 4.03
   b. 43.3
   c. 4.3
2. a. .704
   b. .74
   c. 7.04
3. a. 1.09
   b. 1.19
   c. 1.90
4. a. .613
   b. .630
   c. 600.13
5. a. 3.14
   b. 3.40
   c. 3.040

6. a. .1
   b. .001
   c. .01
7. a. 7.006
   b. 7.060
   c. 7.0006
8. a. .50
   b. 15.1
   c. .15
9. a. 45.9
   b. 45.09
   c. 459.0
10. a. 500.07
    b. .507
    c. .0507

10-6 Equivalent Decimals in Tenths, Hundredths, and Thousandths

Compare	.4	.40	and	.400
	↑	↑		↑
	four tenths	forty hundredths		four hundred thousandths

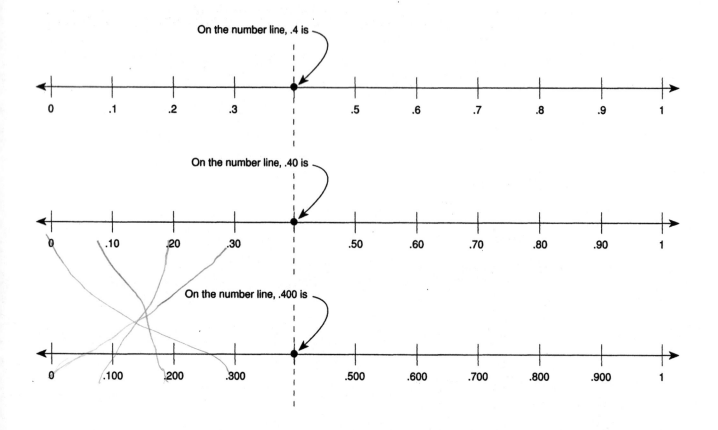

On the number line, .4 is

0 .1 .2 .3 .5 .6 .7 .8 .9 1

On the number line, .40 is

0 .10 .20 .30 .50 .60 .70 .80 .90 1

On the number line, .400 is

0 .100 .200 .300 .500 .600 .700 .800 .900 1

.4 = .40 = .400
They are the *equivalent* decimals.

To change a decimal in *tenths* to an equivalent decimal in *thousandths*, write two more zeros, one in the hundredths' place and one in the thousandths' place:

$$tenths \rightarrow thousandths$$
$$.3 \rightarrow .3\underline{00} \qquad (.3 = .300)$$

To change a decimal in *hundredths* to an equivalent decimal in *thousandths*, write one more zero in the thousandths' place:

$$hundredths \rightarrow thousandths$$
$$1.25 \rightarrow 1.25\underline{0} \qquad (1.25 = 1.250)$$

Exercise 10-F

Write the following decimals as *thousandths*.

1. 7.3 = *7.300*
2. 1.6
3. 17.21
4. 9.0
5. 56.11

6. 2.4
7. 243.2
8. 97.12
9. 51.20
10. 6.91

11. 2.63
12. 193.7
13. 2.67
14. 19.8
15. 1.71

Example:

Compare .7 with .736.

To compare decimals in *tenths* and *thousandths*:

1. Change the decimal in tenths to *thousandths*:

   .7   .736
   ↓
   .700   .736

2. Now, both decimals are in *thousandths*. Compare:

   .700 < .736
          so
   .7   < .736

Example:

Compare .63 with .621.

1. Change .63 to *thousandths*, and compare:

   .63   .621
   ↓
   .630 > .621
            so
   .63   > .621

Exercise 10-G

Compare the decimals. Use <, >, or =.

1. .73 > .725
2. 1.6 ___ 1.614
3. 2.9 ___ 2.891
4. 31.24 ___ 31.239
5. 2.006 ___ 2.6
6. .071 ___ .07
7. 19.3 ___ 19.300
8. .670 ___ .6

9. .41 ___ .419
10. 1.300 ___ 1.3
11. 17.91 ___ 17.199
12. 8.1 ___ 8.111
13. .973 ___ .9
14. .240 ___ .2
15. .100 ___ 1.10
16. 19.014 ___ 19.2

17. 3.066 ___ 4.7
18. .77 ___ .7
19. .6 ___ .60
20. 3.2 ___ 3.19
21. .456 ___ .5
22. .009 ___ .109
23. .98 ___ .9
24. .554 ___ .5

We have studied decimals in

tenths: .2
          3.4   . $\overline{}$
                    ↑
             tenths' place

hundredths: .64
             9.07   . $\overline{}\ \overline{}$
                        ↑
                hundredths' place

thousandths: .774
             9.001   . $\overline{}\ \overline{}\ \overline{}$
                          ↑
                 thousandths' place

There are many *more* decimal places to learn:

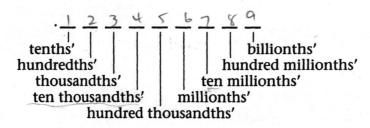

```
tenths'      |  |  |  |  |  |  |  |  billionths'
hundredths'  |  |  |  |  |  |  hundred millionths'
   thousandths'  |  |  |  ten millionths'
   ten thousandths'  |  millionths'
      hundred thousandths'
```

Example:

*What is the **place name** of the number underlined?*

6.32<u>4</u>9

Answer: thousandths' place

Write the *place name* of each number underlined.

1. 6.<u>3</u>974
2. .936<u>4</u>
3. 1.29664<u>1</u>
4. 24.1<u>9</u>36
5. 11.0060<u>1</u>
6. .000016<u>7</u>

7. 4.3<u>0</u>96
8. 2.1467804<u>1</u>
9. 19.24<u>6</u>3
10. 1.3974<u>2</u>
11. 3.<u>2</u>147
12. 6.1589<u>2</u>

13. 103.4<u>9</u>604
14. 72.63214<u>7</u>
15. 2.904<u>0</u>76
16. .4963<u>4</u>2
17. .3<u>4</u>982
18. 17.24673589<u>6</u>

Example:

How do you say or read the decimal 4.3261?

4.326<u>1</u>

The decimal ends in the *ten thousandths'* place. We write or say the decimal as:

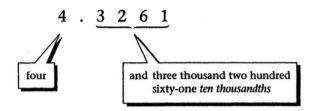

REMEMBER:

We always read the decimal point as *"and."*
We always say the *place name* at the end.

or

We can say: "four point three two six one"

Example:

Write the decimal   2.0004<u>0</u>

The decimal ends in the *hundred thousandths'* place. We write or say the decimal as

"two and forty *hundred thousandths*"

Exercise 10-I

Say the decimals aloud, then write them out.

1. 6.243	6. 6.301	11. 143.6731
2. .0009	7. 14.0000020	12. 2123.4
3. 19.32	8. 6.195	13. 9.00276
4. 9.42610	9. .37	14. 9.000900
5. .00013	10. 195.2	15. .700010

Write as *decimals*.

16. seven and six hundredths
17. two and nine hundred fifty-five thousandths
18. seventy-five ten thousandths
19. eleven and seven tenths
20. nine hundred ninety-five ten millionths
21. one and nine hundredths
22. four thousand sixty-three and nine tenths
23. eighty-two and sixteen hundred thousandths
24. forty and eleven thousandths
25. seven hundred sixty-one and three billionths
26. ninety-eight hundred millionths
27. seventy thousandths
28. six tenths
29. nineteen hundred thousandths
30. two and six hundred fifty thousand millionths

Exercise 10-J

Match the decimal on the left with the correct letter on the right:

1. 4.231 *i*   5 a. two and nineteen hundredths
2. 62   7 b. six and two hundredths
+ 3. 4.0231   3 c. four and two hundred thirty-one ten thousandths
4. 6.2   9 d. two and nineteen thousandths
5. 2.19   11 e. four and two hundred thirty-one ten millionths
6. 4.00231   13 f. two thousand nineteen
7. 6.02   4 g. six and two tenths
8. 6.002   12 h. forty-two thousand three hundred ten
9. 2.019   1 i. four and two hundred thirty-one thousandths
10. 219   14 j. six hundred two
11. 4.0000231   15 k. two and nineteen ten thousandths
12. 42310   10 l. two hundred nineteen
13. 2019   2 m. sixty-two
14. 602   4 n. six and two thousandths
15. 2.0019   6 o. four and two hundred thirty-one hundred thousandths

Write the decimals *in order*, from smallest to greatest.

1. 6.21, .621, 621.0, 6.211, 62.1
2. .0413, .0431, .04013, .0341. .0423
3. .98, 9.2, .99, 9.1, 98.1
4. .88, .8, 8.0, .08, 80.0
5. 7.63, 6.73, .763, 76.3, 67.3
6. 1.271, 12.71, .1271, 127.1, .01271
7. .781, 78.1, 7.81, .718, 78.11
8. .00123, .00321, .0213, .0123, .0321
9. 16.1, .161, 1.61, .016, 1610.0
10. .065, .0065, .056, .0056, .650
11. 5.11, 51.1, .511, .0511, 511.0
12. .998, 9.98, .9978, .099, .989
13. .764, .746, .765, .757, .756
14. .11274, .11724, .11247, .11742, .12741
15. 128.32, 128.23, 182.32, 128.41, 128.14
16. .0719, .0179, .0917, .0799, .0977
17. .3343, .3334, .3344, 3.333, .3333
18. 22.244, 22.424, .2244, 2.244, 22.4243

LET'S TALK ABOUT ...

1. decimals	3. tenths	5. thousandths	7. hundred thousandths
2. decimal point	4. hundredths	6. ten thousandths	8. millionths

Look on the next page and answer the questions or complete the sentences. Write *one* letter in each square to form a word. The words go across → or down ↓.

ACROSS →

1. What is the place name between the ones' place and the hundredths' place?

7. We read the sign in a subtraction problem as _____.

8. What is a prime number less than 20?

10. We _____ a problem when we find the answer to a problem.

11. The number we multiply to get a product is called a _____.

13. ⌢ This is called a decimal _____.

16. The number 3 is not an even number, it is an _____ number.

17. There is no end to a number line. It is _____.

18. A prime number has two factors: the number _____ and itself.

19. We read the sign in an addition problem as _____.

20. ⌢ This is called a _____ point.

2. 0, 2, 4, 6, 8, . . . are called _____ numbers.

3. The answer in an addition problem is called a _____.

4. The answer in a division problem is called a _____.

5. A number between –1 and 1 is _____.

6. The number 6 is _____ than 7.

8. A prime number less than 15 is _____.

9. If two numbers have the same value, they are _____.

12. When we change the number 29 to 30, we are _____ to the nearest tens' place.

13. The answer in a multiplication problem is called a _____.

14. Another word for "two times" is _____.

15. When we multiply a number by 2, we double the number; if we multiply by 3, we _____ the number.

Write with *words*, in two ways.

1. 3.4
2. .74
3. 19.567

4. .875
5. 2.0090
6. .034001

Write as *decimals*.

7. five tenths
8. sixteen thousandths
9. two and three hundredths

10. ten and thirty ten thousandths
11. seven hundred sixty millionths
12. thirty hundred thousandths

Write the *place names* of the numbers underlined.

13. .4<u>5</u>7
14. 3.95<u>8</u>4
15. 3.<u>5</u>

16. .245684<u>9</u>
17. .5674<u>3</u>
18. .00000<u>1</u>

19. 144.334<u>5</u>
20. .<u>4</u>7566
21. 67.7<u>8</u>55

Compare the decimals. Use <, >, or =.

22. 5.6 ___ 5.63
23. .45 ___ .450
24. 34.607 ___ 34.660
25. 5.45 ___ 5.4
26. .567 ___ .6

27. .5900 ___ .59
28. .670 ___ .6710
29. .878 ___ .91
30. .129 ___ .1290
31. 8.23 < 9.20

32. 4.556 ___ 4.55
33. .449 ___ .45
34. .6700 ___ .670
35. .7112 ___ .71121
36. 1.009 > 1.0010

11 Adding and Subtracting Decimals

11-1 Writing Integers as Decimals

We can write any integer as a decimal. We write a decimal point to the right of the integer and one or more zeros:

Integer		Decimal
3	→	3.0
		3.00
		3.000
		etc.

$$3 = 3.0 = 3.00 = 3.000 \ldots$$

These are all *equivalent* decimals. We can write any number of zeros after the decimal point. It does not change the value of the decimal.

Example:

Write 62 as a decimal ending in the thousandths' place.

$$62 \rightarrow 62.000$$

Since we want the decimal to end in the *thousandths'* place, we write a decimal point and three zeros. We read the decimal as "sixty-two" or "sixty-two point zero zero zero."

Exercise 11-A

Write as decimals ending in the:

tenths' place	hundredths' place	thousandths' place:
1. 16	7. 24	13. 63
2. 9	8. 10	14. 7
3. 1	9. 365	15. 21
4. 122	10. 2	16. 724
5. 89	11. 926	17. 90
6. 12	12. 1,341	18. 4,230

Example:

$$7 + 3.2 + 1.6$$

1. Rewrite the decimals so that the decimal points are *in line*. Change the integer 7 to a decimal ending in the *tenths'* place, since 3.2 and 1.6 end in the tenths' place.

$$
\begin{array}{r}
7.0 \\
3.2 \\
+\ 1.6 \\
\hline
\end{array}
$$
↑
decimal points *in line*

2. Then add:

$$
\begin{array}{r}
7.0 \\
3.2 \\
+\ 1.6 \\
\hline
\end{array}
$$
Answer: 11.8

Example:

$$4.2 + 21.32 + 12$$

Line up the decimal points. Since 21.32 ends in the *hundredths'* place, we write 4.2 to end in the *hundredths'* place (4.20) and we write 12 to end in the *hundredths'* place (12.00):

$$
\begin{array}{r}
4.20 \\
21.32 \\
+\ \ 12.00 \\
\hline
\end{array}
$$
Answer: 37.52
↑
decimal points *in line*

Exercise 11-B

Rewrite the decimals and add.

1. $6.3 + .9 + 4.7$
2. $17.27 + 8.83 + .96$
3. $317.29 + 19.56 + .74$
4. $.86 + 92 + 8.2$

5. $7.4 + 11 + .19$
6. $.236 + 1.4 + 8$
7. $14.1 + 82.47 + .9$
8. $7.6 + 2 + 1.105$

9. 4.34 + .793 + 6

10. 8.8 + .75 + 14.2

11. 19.3 + .145 + 89

12. 7.5 + 845 + 16.97

13. .54 + 11 + 1.9

14. .9 + 12.6 + 144 + 6

15. 62.4 + 12 + 8.6 + .7

16. 473 + 26.9 + .14 + .23

17. 4 + 6.3 + .27 + .8

18. .896 + 72 + 1.3 + .11

19. 2.975 + .26 + 84 + .95

20. 95.4 + .237 + 8.6 + 54

21. 62.4 + 9 + .596

22. .0071 + 13 + 2.43 + .4

23. 16.32 + 9.2 + .334 + 2

24. 75 + .263 + 1.1 + .556

25. .45 + 9.9 + 181.3 + .65

26. .29 + 4.6 + 23 + .01

27. 4.312 + .8 + 7.15 + .49

28. 88.9 + 176.4 + 16 + .5

29. 2.223 + .0021 + .45 + 33

30. .453 + 6 + 5.44 + .077 + 22

Exercise 11-C   Problem Solving: TOURING!

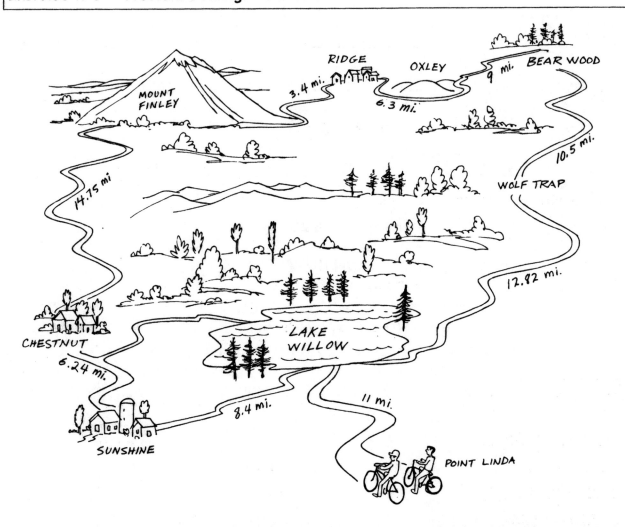

Mario and Gus went on a bicycle trip around Sunset Canyon and Lake Willow last month. The boys began their tour at Point Linda. Answer the questions below. Show all of your work!

1. Mario and Gus began their trip at Point Linda on a Sunday. They bicycled to Lake Willow, then on to Chestnut. How many miles did they travel on Sunday?

2. On Monday, the boys rode from Chestnut to Mount Finley, then they returned to Chestnut that evening. How many miles was this altogether?

3. Gus wanted to visit Bear Wood on Tuesday. They rode from Chestnut.
   a. Which way was closer: from Chestnut to Bear Wood through Mount Finley, or from Chestnut to Bear Wood through Lake Willow?
   b. How much closer (in miles) was this route?

4. On Wednesday, the boys spent a day and a night at Lake Willow for fishing and swimming. Then on Thursday, they rode to Oxley, then back to Wolf Trap, where they had dinner. How many miles did they ride on Thursday?

5. On Friday, Mario rode from Wolf Trap to Mount Finley, through Bear Wood. Gus rode from Wolf Trap to Mount Finley, through Lake Willow. Who arrived there sooner, Mario or Gus?

6. Before they returned home, the boys rode from Lake Willow and toured all around Sunset Canyon, then back to Lake Willow. What were the total miles for this ride?

11-3 | Money

We use decimals to express money. Paper money, or bills, are called *dollars*:

one dollar = $1.00
two dollars = $2.00
three dollars = $3.00
etc.

Coins are called *cents*:

one penny = one hundredth of a dollar
= $ .01 (we say "one cent")
one nickel = five hundredths of a dollar
= $ .05 (we say "five cents")
one dime = ten hundredths of a dollar
= $ .10 (we say "ten cents")
one quarter = twenty-five hundredths of a dollar
= $ .25 (we say "twenty- five cents")
one half-dollar = fifty hundredths of a dollar
= $ .50 (we say "fifty cents")

Example:

Read aloud, or write: $1.24

"one dollar and twenty-four cents"

or

"one twenty-four"

Exercise 11-D

Read aloud, or write with words.

1. $3.45	6. $15.95	11. $100.00
2. $.15	7. $.99	12. $345.55
3. $4.50	8. $35.66	13. $560.80
4. $.95	9. $75.25	14. $888.88
5. $10.00	10. $19.99	15. $744.98

Example:

$.18 = 18 pennies   (18 coins)
    or   3 nickels and 3 pennies (6 coins)
    or   1 dime, 1 nickel and 3 pennies (5 coins)
This combination of coins (5 coins) shows the *least* number of coins that we can use to express $.18.

Example:

$.76 = 76 pennies   (76 coins)
    or   7 dimes, 1 nickel, and 1 penny (9 coins)
    or   3 quarters and 1 penny   (4 coins)
    or   1 half-dollar, 1 quarter, and 1 penny (3 coins)
This combination of coins (3 coins) shows the *least* number of coins that we can use to express $.76.

List the combinations of coins for each amount. Use the *least* number of coins:

	Pennies	Nickels	Dimes	Quarters	Half-dollars	Total coins
1. $.13	3	–	1	–	–	4
2. $.68						
3. $.59						
4. $.95						
5. $.27						
6. $.82						
7. $.99						
8. $.47						
9. $.62						
10. $.70						
11. $.34						
12. $.69						
13. $.78						
14. $.19						
15. $.91						

Exercise 11-F   Problem Solving: TOURING EXPENSES!

Mario and Gus slept at a campground in Chestnut for three nights.

1. The campground charges $18.00 per person for one night. For others in the same group, they charge $8.00 per person for each night.
   a. How much did Mario and Gus pay for one night?
   b. How much did they pay for three nights?

2. The boys ate breakfast, lunch, and dinner at the Cafe Chestnut. Here are their food bills:

	Breakfast	Lunch	Dinner
Day 1	$7.25	$8.95	$12.80
Day 2	$6.95	$9.33	$10.55
Day 3	$8.25	$10.15	$ 9.36

   a. How much did they pay for breakfast for 3 days?
   b. How much did they pay for lunch for 3 days?
   c. How much did they pay for dinner for 3 days?
   d. Did they spend more money for breakfast, lunch, and dinner on day 2 or day 3?
   e. What was their *total* food bill for all 3 days?

3. Additional expenses for the trip included:

Bicycle tires	$18.00
First-aid kit	$23.50
Extra food for trip	$19.85

How much did they pay for the additional expenses?

4. How much did they spend altogether for the campground, food, and additional expenses?

5. The boys had $250 to spend. How much money did they have left over after the trip?

11-4 | Subtracting Decimals

Example:

$$6 - 4.3$$

Rewrite the decimals so that the decimal points are *in line*. Change the integer 6 to a decimal ending in the *tenths'* place, since 4.3 ends in the tenths' place. Then subtract:

$$\begin{array}{r} 6.0 \\ - 4.3 \\ \hline 1.7 \end{array}$$

Answer: 1.7

Example:

$$.6 - .3211$$

Rewrite the decimals so the decimal points are *in line*. Since .3211 is a decimal ending in the *ten thousandths'* place, we must write .6 as a decimal ending in the *ten thousandths'* place. We write 3 more zeros: .6000. Now we subtract:

$$\begin{array}{r} .6000 \\ - .3211 \\ \hline .2789 \end{array}$$

Answer: .2789

Rewrite the decimals and subtract.

1. 43.6 – 3.2	11. 60.03 – 5.69	21. 7 – .334
2. 95.6 – 14.7	12. 42 – 15.89	22. 11 – 3.67
3. 6.3 – 3.8	13. 32 – 12.11	23. .5 – .0012
4. 78.4 – 19.9	14. 1.8 – .97	24. 45 – 3.8765
5. 24 – 5.8	15. .765 – .349	25. .71 – .3334
6. 135 – 24.7	16. .6 – .489	26. 3 – .177
7. 39.6 – 12	17. 5.6 – .89	27. 19.766 – .3
8. 53 – 43.8	18. .4 – .398	28. 97.5 – 12
9. 130.64 – 15.9	19. .97 – .499	29. 51 – .2344
10. 17.2 – 14	20. .3 – .296	30. 4.111 – .99

11-5 Using Inverse Operations to Find Missing Decimals

We used inverse operations to find missing *numbers* in Chapter 5. We can use inverse operations to find missing *decimals*.

Example:

$$\_\_ - 3.5 = .67$$

Use the inverse operation:

$$.67 + 3.5 = 4.17$$

Answer: $4.17 - 3.5 = .67$

Example:

$$2.34 + \_\_\_ = 7.5$$

Use the inverse operation:

$$7.5 - 2.34 = 5.16$$

Answer: $2.34 + 5.16 = 7.5$

Use the *inverse operation* to find the missing numbers.

1. $3.45 + \underline{\hphantom{xx}} = 4.33$

2. $\underline{\hphantom{xx}} + .224 = 2.33$

3. $\underline{\hphantom{xx}} - 4.5 = 10.6$

4. $.345 + \underline{\hphantom{xx}} = 1.99$

5. $\underline{\hphantom{xx}} - .39 = 5.67$

6. $\underline{\hphantom{xx}} - .23 = 12.44$

7. $8.76 + \underline{\hphantom{xx}} = 19.7$

8. $\underline{\hphantom{xx}} - .87 = 8$

9. $\underline{\hphantom{xx}} - 1.22 = .99$

10. $6 + \underline{\hphantom{xx}} = 23.86$

11. $\underline{\hphantom{xx}} + 23.445 = 67.5$

12. $\underline{\hphantom{xx}} - 3.89 = 5$

13. $\underline{\hphantom{xx}} - 6 = 8.67$

14. $.54 + \underline{\hphantom{xx}} = 3.666$

15. $.234 + \underline{\hphantom{xx}} = 7$

16. $\underline{\hphantom{xx}} - .233 = .112$

17. $\underline{\hphantom{xx}} - 7.66 = 2.389$

18. $\underline{\hphantom{xx}} - .293 = 1.245$

19. $1.23 + \underline{\hphantom{xx}} = 3.44$

20. $\underline{\hphantom{xx}} + .334 = 198.3$

21. $\underline{\hphantom{xx}} - .983 = 2.12$

22. $\underline{\hphantom{xx}} + .231 = 4.55$

23. $\underline{\hphantom{xx}} + .345 = .67$

24. $\underline{\hphantom{xx}} - 13.2 = 2.56$

25. $\underline{\hphantom{xx}} - 8 = 2.33$

26. $\underline{\hphantom{xx}} + .12 = .34$

27. $45 + \underline{\hphantom{xx}} = 65.00$

28. $\underline{\hphantom{xx}} - .243 = 5$

29. $\underline{\hphantom{xx}} - 8.34 = 0$

30. $.191 + \underline{\hphantom{xx}} = .191$

Exercise 11-I   GET IN SHAPE!

The members of Peter U's Health Club want to lose weight. Look at their weights for 3 weeks:

Name	Week 1	Week 2	Week 3
Carl Lewison	184.34 pounds	180.26 pounds	176.24 pounds
Ben Jackson	219.26 pounds	224.16 pounds	221.32 pounds
Jackie Joyful	148.29 pounds	153.64 pounds	54.26 pounds
Dwight Stony	174.55 pounds	171.24 pounds	170.06 pounds
Dorothy Hamilton	139.65 pounds	134.21 pounds	132.19 pounds

1. Look at week 1. Who weighs more, Jackie Joyful or Dorothy Hamilton?

2. How much more?

3. Look at Carl Lewison's weights. How much did he lose from week 1 to week 3?

4. Did Ben Jackson gain or lose weight from week 1 to week 2?

5. How much weight?

6. How much weight did Dwight Stony lose from week 1 to week 2?

7. How much weight did Dwight Stony lose from week 1 to week 3?

8. Carl Lewison weighs less than Ben Jackson. Look at their weights in week 3. How much less does Carl Lewison weigh?

9. Add all the weights for week 1 and compare that number with all of the weights for week 3. What is the difference?

10. Compare Dorothy Hamilton's weight in week 1 with Ben Jackson's weight in week 3. What is the difference?

11. Which two combined weights are closest to 400 pounds?
    Group 1: Carl Lewison's and Ben Jackson's weights in week 3.
    Group 2: Ben Jackson's and Dwight Stony's weights in week 2.

12. How many more pounds are needed to equal 400 pounds for
    a. Group 1?
    b. Group 2?

11-6 Rounding Off Decimals

We learned how to round off *numbers* in Chapter 3. We round off *decimals* in the same way.

Example:

Round off 1.38 to the nearest **tenths'** *place.*

1. Underline the *tenths'* place digit and look at the number to the right:

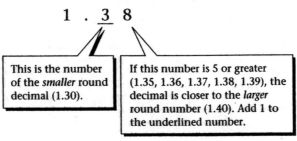

$$1.\cancel{3}\cancel{8} \rightarrow 1.40$$

2. We are rounding to the nearest *tenths'* place, so we want the decimal to end in the *tenths'* place. We must drop all the numbers after the tenths' digit.

$$1.4\cancel{0} \rightarrow 1.4$$

Answer: $1.38 \rightarrow 1.4$

Example:

Round off 5.0132 to the nearest **hundredths'** *place.*

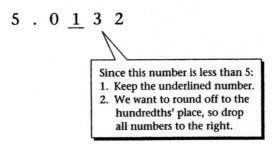

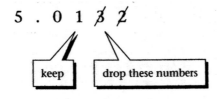

Answer: $5.0132 \rightarrow 5.01$

Example:

Round off 5.978 to the nearest **tenths' place.**

5 . <u>9</u> 7 8

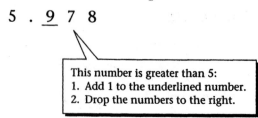

This number is greater than 5:
1. Add 1 to the underlined number.
2. Drop the numbers to the right.

$$5 . 9\ 7\ 8 \quad \rightarrow \quad \overset{6}{\not{5}} . \overset{0}{\not{9}}\ 7\ 8$$

Answer: 5.978 → 6.0

Example:

Round 3.6 to the nearest **whole number.**

Underline the *ones'* place digit.

<u>3</u> . 6

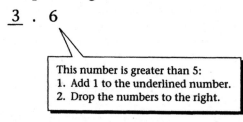

This number is greater than 5:
1. Add 1 to the underlined number.
2. Drop the numbers to the right.

Answer: 3.6 → 4

Exercise 11-J

Round off to the nearest *tenths'* place.

1. 6.12	6. 7.613	11. 6.692
2. 24.35	7. 2.188	12. 49.573
3. 19.87	8. 49.54	13. 1.845
4. 2.317	9. 3.96	14. 3.788
5. 1.96	10. 4.773	15. 2.556

Round off to the nearest *hundredths'* place.

16. 34.723	21. 1.339	26. 3.5643
17. 3.677	22. 243.5921	27. 11.432
18. 4.782	23. 36.995	28. 45.009
19. 11.941	24. 7.9421	29. 33.999
20. 2.6971	25. 42.641	30. 1.2388

Round off to the nearest *whole number*.

1. 7.34	6. 21.44	11. 7.256
2. 9.58	7. 8.34	12. 9.827
3. 2.98	8. 7.66	13. 9.82
4. 9.21	9. 2.554	14. 30.78
5. 1.80	10. 9.05	15. 21.80

Round to the nearest *thousandths'* place.

16. 4.3987	21. 165.92655	26. 8.21098
17. 32.51223	22. 1.22344	27. 11.40032
18. 7.4998	23. 2.00833	28. .29384
19. 21.92336	24. 12.38054	29. .11354
20. 5.45788	25. 29.6744	30. .289939

LET'S TALK ABOUT ...

1. money	6. nickel
2. bill	7. dime
3. coin	8. quarter
4. cent	9. half dollar
5. penny	10. dollar

Rewrite the decimals and *add*.

1. .45 + 5 + 12.2
2. 10.33 + 2.4 + 2
3. 45 + 4.5 + .45
4. 193.4 + 2.77 + .5

5. 98.33 + 75 + 23.3
6. 15.33 + 567 + .002
7. 25 + 334 + .544
8. 205.35 + .677 + 49

Rewrite the decimals and *subtract*.

9 3.56 – 2.44
10. 5.67 – 4.8
11. .334 – .23
12. 2.4 – .33

13. 86 – 3.67
14. 12 – .005
15. 3 – 2.56
16. 265.34 – 9.445

Use the inverse operations to solve.

17. 94.3 + ___ = 122.67
18. ___ – .334 = 12.3

19. ___ – 1.76 = 1.76
20. ___ + .867 = 1.223

Round off to the nearest *tenths'* place.

21. 3.54
22. 127.89
23. 12.993

24. .318
25. 19.056
26. 2.104

Round off to the nearest *hundredths'* and *thousandths'* places.

	Hundredths'		Thousandths'
27. 27.3512	_____	29.	_____
28. 3.7597	_____	30.	_____

12 Multiplying and Dividing Decimals

12-1 Multiplying Decimals

Look at the following three problems.

$$\text{(a)} \quad \begin{array}{r} 25 \\ \times \ 4 \end{array} \qquad \text{(b)} \quad \begin{array}{r} 2.5 \\ \times \ 4 \end{array} \qquad \text{(c)} \quad \begin{array}{r} .25 \\ \times \ 4 \end{array}$$

The numbers in all three problems are the same, but in (b) there is a decimal point between the 2 and 5, and in (c) there is a decimal point before the 2. Will the answers be *different* for all three problems?

In problem (a):
$$\begin{array}{r} 25 \\ \times \ 4 \\ \hline 100 \end{array}$$

There are *no* decimal points in (a). The answer is 100.

In problem (b):
$$\begin{array}{r} 2.5 \\ \times \ 4 \end{array}$$

We are multiplying 4 by a decimal *greater* than 2 and *less* than 3, since 2.5 is between 2 and 3.

$$\left.\begin{array}{l} 4 \times 2 = 8 \\ 4 \times 3 = 12 \end{array}\right\} \quad \text{The answer should be between 8 and 12.}$$

$$\begin{array}{r} 2.5 \\ \times \ 4 \\ \hline 10.0 \end{array} \quad \text{The answer is 10.}$$

In problem (c):
$$\begin{array}{r} .25 \\ \times \ 4 \end{array}$$

We are multiplying 4 by a decimal *less* than 1 (.25). The answer should be *less* than 4:

$$\begin{array}{r} .25 \\ \times \ 4 \\ \hline 1.00 \end{array} \quad \text{The answer is 1.}$$

In problems (a), (b), and (c) the numbers were the same, but the decimal points changed the value of the numbers and answers:

(a) 25	(b) 2.5	(c) .25
× 4	× 4	× 4
100	10.0	1.00

When multiplying with decimals, we must *never* forget the decimal points!

In problem (b):

2.5 ← There is one number (5) to the right of the decimal point.
× 4
10.0 ← The answer also shows one number to the right of the decimal point.

In problem (c):

.25 ← There are two numbers to the right of the decimal point.
× 4
1.00 ← The answer also shows two numbers to the right of the decimal point.

WHEN MULTIPLYING WITH DECIMALS:

1. Multiply the numbers together.

2. Count how many numbers are to the right of the decimal point(s) in each factor.

3. Place the decimal point in the answer so that there are the *same* number of numbers to the right of the decimal point as in the factors.

Example:

12.3 ← 1 number to the right of the point.
× 3
36.9 ← 1 number to the right of the point.

1.23 ← 2 numbers.
× 3
3.69 ← 2 numbers (count 2 places to the left ← and write the decimal point).

1.23 ← 2 numbers.
× .3 ← +1 number.
.369 ← 3 numbers (count 3 places to the left ← and write the decimal point).

Sometimes we must add zeros:

$$
\begin{array}{r}
.123 \\
\times \quad .3 \\
\hline
.0369 \\
\end{array}
\quad
\begin{array}{l}
\leftarrow \quad 3 \text{ numbers.} \\
\leftarrow \underline{+\,1} \text{ number.} \\
\leftarrow \quad 4 \text{ numbers (count 4 places to the left, write} \\
\qquad \text{in a 0 and write the decimal point).}
\end{array}
$$

$$
\begin{array}{r}
.0123 \\
\times \quad .03 \\
\hline
.000369 \\
\end{array}
\quad
\begin{array}{l}
\leftarrow \quad 4 \text{ numbers.} \\
\leftarrow \underline{+\,2} \text{ numbers.} \\
\leftarrow \quad 6 \text{ numbers (count 6 places to the left, write} \\
\qquad \text{in 3 zeroes and write the decimal point).}
\end{array}
$$

Example:

Count how many numbers are to the right of each factor, then place the decimal point in the answers:

(a)	.45	(b)	.45	(c)	.045
	× .4		× .04		× .004
	180		180		180

Answers: (a) .180   (b) .0180   (c) .000180

Exercise 12-A

Rewrite each answer, placing the decimal point in the correct place.

1.	3.4	5.	.0034	9.	.2456	13.	16.30
	× 4		× .004		× .004		× .02
	136		136		9824		3260

2.	.34	6.	245.6	10.	.2456	14.	.63
	× 4		× 4		× .0004		× .23
	136		9824		9824		1449

3.	.034	7.	24.56	11.	1630	15.	100
	× .4		× .04		× .2		× .3
	136		9824		3260		300

4.	.034	8.	2.456	12.	163.0	16.	1.00
	× .04		× .04		× .2		× .03
	136		9824		3260		300

17.
```
     572
  ×   33
   18876
```

19.
```
    .572
  ×  .33
   18876
```

21.
```
   234
 ×  .1
   234
```

23.
```
   2.34
 ×  .01
    234
```

18.
```
    5.72
  ×  .33
   18876
```

20.
```
    .0572
  ×  .033
   18876
```

22.
```
   23.4
 ×  .01
    234
```

24.
```
    .0234
 ×   .001
      234
```

Exercise 12-B

Multiply the decimals.

1.
```
   16.5
 ×    2
```

11.
```
   3.400
 ×    23
```

21.
```
   .3298
 ×   .33
```

2.
```
   34.23
 ×    .3
```

12.
```
   96.40
 ×  .008
```

22.
```
   .0023
 ×   .13
```

3.
```
   12.34
 ×    .5
```

13.
```
   23.98
 ×     5
```

23.
```
   .1223
 ×   .03
```

4.
```
   2.678
 ×    .2
```

14.
```
    1198
 ×    .2
```

24.
```
   3.455
 ×   .87
```

5.
```
   .376
 × .02
```

15.
```
   .67
 × .78
```

25.
```
   1.003
 ×  .012
```

6.
```
   .238
 ×  .3
```

16.
```
   .045
 × .99
```

26.
```
   3.122
 ×  .766
```

7.
```
   2.009
 ×   .05
```

17.
```
   1.200
 ×   .20
```

27.
```
   123.4
 ×  .002
```

8.
```
   .1900
 ×    .1
```

18.
```
   100.0
 ×   .10
```

28.
```
   9882.1
 ×   .009
```

9.
```
   .45
 × .56
```

19.
```
   3.445
 ×    .3
```

29.
```
   1.2665
 ×   .011
```

10.
```
   .988
 × .34
```

20.
```
   4.98
 × .76
```

30.
```
   .33444
 ×  .112
```

Rita goes to college and works part time as a cashier at the **International Market**.

1. Rita earns $8.45 an hour at the **International Market**. Look at her work schedule each week:

Monday	Tuesday	Wednesday	Thursday	Friday	Saturday
4 hours	5 hours	5 hours	5 hours	5 hours	8 hours

   a. How many hours does Rita work in 1 week?
   b. How much money does she earn in 1 week?
   c. The government takes out $41.50 a week in taxes from Rita's paycheck, so her paycheck is $41.50 less each week. What is her *take-home* pay (the amount of money she receives after taxes) each week?
   d. There are 4 weeks in a month. What is Rita's *take-home* pay for 1 month?
   e. What is her *take-home* pay for 1 year?

2. Rita is renting an apartment for $375.00 a month. She also pays about $16.50 each month for gas and $19.75 a month for electricity. Her telephone bill is about $21.75 a month. She pays $55.50 a month for college tuition. Complete her expenses for 1 month and for 1 year:

	For 1 month	For 1 year
a. rent	_____	_____
b. gas	_____	_____
c. electricity	_____	_____
d. telephone	_____	_____
e. tuition	_____	_____
total:	_____	total: _____

3. How much does Rita have left over each month after she pays all of her bills? (Use her *take-home* pay as her monthly salary.)

1. One Saturday, Mrs. Li bought the following items. Look at the illustration on the next page for the price of each item and complete the list below (lb = pound).

Item	Price	Amount	Total Cost
a. bean sprouts	$.65	3.6 lb	.65 x 3.6 = $2.340 = $2.34
b. kiwi	_____	2 lb	_____
c. salmon	_____	2.5 lb	_____
d. potatoes	_____	6 lb	_____
e. Fuji apples	_____	2.8 lb	_____
f. duck	_____	1.4 lb	_____
g. squid	_____	2.6 lb	_____
h. platanos	_____	3 lb	_____
i. mackerel	_____	3.2 lb	_____

2. What was Mrs. Li's total bill?

3. Mrs. Li gave Rita $75.00. How much change did Rita give Mrs. Li?

Exercise 12-E   MORE SHOPPING!

The next week, all prices changed. Some prices *increased,* and some prices *decreased*:

Increase per pound		Decrease per pound	
kiwi	+ $.25	platanos	– $.73
Fuji apples	+ $.39	napa	– $.74
bean sprouts	+ $.15	duck	– $1.19
chayote	+ $.08	mackerel	– $.93
potatoes	+ $.13		
chicken parts	+ $.27		
squid	+ $1.00		
salmon	+ $1.27		

1. Mrs. Li bought the items below. Complete the list with the new information. *Round off* to the nearest *cent* (hundredths' place).

Item	New Price	Amount	Total Cost
a. potatoes	$.49 + .13 = $.62	3.24 lb	3.24 x .62 = $2.0088 = $2.01
b. chayote	_____	4.13 lb	_____
c. chicken parts	_____	6.74 lb	_____
d. duck	_____	1.25 lb	_____
e. mackerel	_____	1.5 lb	_____

f. kiwi	_____	.90 lb	_____
g. platanos	_____	3.82 lb	_____
h. bean sprouts	_____	1.55 lb	_____
i. napa	_____	2.33 lb	_____

2. What was the total bill for the items above?

3. Mrs. Li gave Rita $50.00. How much change did Rita give to Mrs. Li?

12-2 | Multiplying Decimals by Multiples of Ten

We learned how to multiply numbers by multiples of ten quickly. We wrote zeros at the end of the number:

$$34 \times 100 = 3{,}400$$

$$75 \times 10^4 = 750{,}000$$

When we multiply *decimals* by multiples of ten, we *move* the *decimal point* to the right →.

Example:

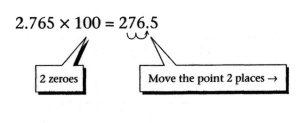

$$2.765 \times 100 = 276.5$$

2 zeroes   Move the point 2 places →

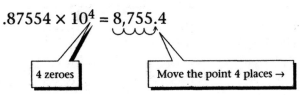

$$.87554 \times 10^4 = 8{,}755.4$$

4 zeroes   Move the point 4 places →

Example:

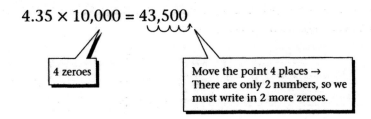

$$4.35 \times 10{,}000 = 43{,}500$$

4 zeroes   Move the point 4 places →
There are only 2 numbers, so we must write in 2 more zeroes.

Multiply the decimals by moving the decimal point.

1. 1.23×100
2. $.445 \times 10$
3. $.54 \times 1,000$
4. $23.456 \times 10,000$
5. 19×100
6. 2.387×100
7. $.45 \times 100,000$
8. 198.1×100
9. 23.4×10
10. $.755 \times 10,000$
11. $2.389 \times 100,000$
12. $3.4 \times 100,000$
13. 29.876×10
14. $19.4 \times 10,000$
15. $123.678 \times 1,000,000$
16. 123.678×10
17. $9.2 \times 1,000,000$
18. $745.30 \times 1,000$
19. $.33948 \times 100$
20. $.00002 \times 10$

Multiply.

21. 17.3×10^1
22. 14.345×10^3
23. 6.114×10^2
24. $.1134 \times 10^3$
25. $.01145 \times 10^4$
26. 67.392×10^5
27. 42.3×10^3
28. $.413 \times 10^5$
29. $.413 \times 10^6$
30. $.413 \times 10^1$
31. 67.1432×10^4
32. 14.21×10^3
33. 1.21×10^5
34. $.666 \times 10^2$
35. $.666 \times 10^6$
36. $.49238 \times 10^2$
37. 2345.3×10^4
38. 34.596×10^1
39. 3.456×10^0
40. 2938.4×10^4

12-3 Dividing with Decimals

Look at the following three problems:

(a) $2 \overline{)184}$ (b) $2 \overline{)18.4}$ (c) $.2 \overline{)184}$

The numbers in all three problems are the same, but in (a) there are *no* decimal points, in (b) there is a decimal point in the *dividend*, and in (c) there is a decimal point in the *divisor*. Will the answers be different for all three problems?

In problem (a): $2\overline{)184}$ quotient 92

There are no decimal points. The answer is 92.

In problem (b): $2\overline{)18.4}$

We are dividing 18.4 (a decimal between 18 and 19) by 2. The answer should be about 9 or a little greater than 9.

$$2\overline{)18.4} \quad \text{quotient } 9.2 \qquad \text{The answer is 9.2}$$

In problem (c): $.2\overline{)184}$

We are dividing 184 by a decimal much less than 1 (.2 < 1). So the answer should be much greater than 184, since 184 divided by 1 equals 184.

$$.2\overline{)184} \quad \text{quotient } 920 \qquad \text{The answer is 920.}$$

In problems (a), (b), and (c) the numbers were the same, but the decimal points changed the value of the numbers and answers.

(a) $2\overline{)184}$ quotient 92 (b) $2\overline{)18.4}$ quotient 9.2 (c) $.2\overline{)184}$ quotient 920

When dividing with decimals, we must *never* forget the decimal points!

12-4   If the Dividend Is a Decimal

Example:

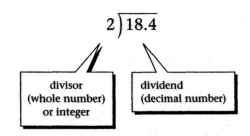

175

When the dividend is a *decimal number*, the quotient will also be a *decimal number*. So we must first rewrite the decimal point *above* ↑ to the quotient:

$$2 \overline{)18.4}$$

Now we can divide:

$$
\begin{array}{r}
9.2 \\
2 \overline{)18.4} \\
-18 \\
\hline
0\,4 \\
-4 \\
\hline
0
\end{array}
$$

Example:

$$5 \overline{).1305}$$

Rewrite the decimal point *above* ↑ to the quotient and divide:

$$
\begin{array}{r}
.0261 \\
5 \overline{)\!.1305} \\
-10 \\
\hline
30 \\
-30 \\
\hline
05 \\
-5 \\
\hline
0
\end{array}
$$

Exercise 12-G

Divide the following.

1. 1.24 ÷ 2	8. 84.7 ÷ 7	15. 727.8 ÷ 6
2. 64.2 ÷ 2	9. 106.4 ÷ 4	16. .9891 ÷ 7
3. 95.5 ÷ 5	10. .40085 ÷ 5	17. 2.124 ÷ 3
4. .168 ÷ 8	11. 698.36 ÷ 4	18. .2124 ÷ 3
5. 23.4 ÷ 6	12. .18720 ÷ 9	19. 212.4 ÷ 3
6. 2.008 ÷ 2	13. 1,201.2 ÷ 6	20. 4.788 ÷ 4
7. 1.988 ÷ 2	14. 24.064 ÷ 8	21. 416.06 ÷ 71

22. .00518 ÷ 37   27. 43.550 ÷ 25   32. 9.725 ÷ 25

23. 5,198.7 ÷ 43   28. 10.490 ÷ 10   33. 28.226 ÷ 22

24. .56400 ÷ 50   29. .03045 ÷ 15   34. .702 ÷ 18

25. 7.5600 ÷ 16   30. 147.960 ÷ 30   35. 479.550 ÷ 75

26. .01095 ÷ 15   31. 152.685 ÷ 65   36. 321.600 ÷ 80

12-5 If the Divisor Is a Decimal

Example:

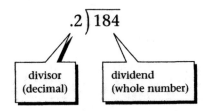

It will be easier if we divide by a *whole number* instead of a decimal number. But we cannot just erase the decimal point in the divisor. We can move the point to the right *one place* (remember, this is the same as multiplying by 10):

$$2.$$

But if we multiply the divisor by 10, we must also multiply the dividend by 10 (this is the same as writing in one zero at the end of the number):

$$\downarrow$$
$$1840$$

$$.2\overline{)184} \rightarrow 2.\overline{)1840}$$

Now divide:

$$
\begin{array}{r}
920 \\
2.\overline{)1840} \\
-18 \\
\overline{04} \\
-4 \\
\overline{00} \\
-0 \\
\overline{0}
\end{array}
$$

Example:

$$.04 \overline{)8}$$

1. Move the decimal point to the right *2 places* (multiplying by 100):

   04.

2. Multiply the dividend by 100 also. (Write in two zeros).

   $$800$$

   $$.04 \overline{)8} \quad \rightarrow \quad 04. \overline{)800}$$

3. Now divide:

   $$
   \begin{array}{r}
   200 \\
   04. \overline{)800} \\
   -8 \\
   \hline
   00 \\
   -0 \\
   \hline
   0
   \end{array}
   $$

Exercise 12-H

Divide the following.

1. 15 ÷ .3	13. 45 ÷ .5	25. 26 ÷ .004
2. 35 ÷ .5	14. 42 ÷ .6	26. 261 ÷ .3
3. 21 ÷ .07	15. 348 ÷ .02	27. 4 ÷ .005
4. 40 ÷ .8	16. 28 ÷ .04	28. 42 ÷ .60
5. 66 ÷ .2	17. 150 ÷ .30	29. 35 ÷ .050
6. 13 ÷ .01	18. 10 ÷ .20	30. 385 ÷ .07
7. 4 ÷ .05	19. 2 ÷ .1	31. 12 ÷ .0004
8. 1506 ÷ .3	20. 6 ÷ .12	32. 364 ÷ .04
9. 920 ÷ .04	21. 21 ÷ .7	33. 2,970 ÷ .090
10. 15 ÷ .10	22. 54 ÷ .90	34. 1,260 ÷ .30
11. 5 ÷ .25	23. 720 ÷ .008	35. 322 ÷ .0002
12. 81 ÷ .9	24. 25 ÷ .20	36. 322 ÷ .02

Example:

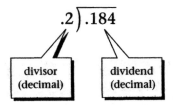

$$.2 \overline{).184}$$

divisor (decimal) dividend (decimal)

Again, it is easier to divide by a *whole number* instead of a decimal number. To change .2 to a whole number, we move the decimal point to the right *1 place* (which is the same as multiplying .2 by 10). Then we must multiply the dividend .184 by 10 also (move the decimal point to the right 1 place):

$$.2.\overline{).1.84}$$

Rewrite the decimal point above ↑ to the quotient and divide:

```
       .92
.2.) .1↑84
     − 1 8
        04
       − 4
         0
```

Example:

$$.12 \overline{).6}$$

1. Write .12 as a whole number (move the decimal point to the right 2 places).

2. Move the decimal point of the dividend 2 places to the right. The dividend .6 has only one digit, so we must write in one zero:

$$.12.\overline{).60.}$$

3. Rewrite the decimal point in the dividend above ↑ to the quotient and divide:

```
          5.
.12.) .60↑
      − 60
         0
```

Divide the following.

1. 21.6 ÷ .6	13. 175.6 ÷ .004	25. 145.920 ÷ .60
2. .117 ÷ .9	14. 1.5 ÷ .25	26. 2.8864 ÷ .04
3. 40.56 ÷ .8	15. 1.2 ÷ .30	27. .325260 ÷ .006
4. 7.2 ÷ .8	16. 6.0 ÷ .10	28. 3.544 ÷ .02
5. .1506 ÷ .3	17. 3.0 ÷ 1.5	29. 11.5025 ÷ 4.3
6. .0384 ÷ .4	18. 14.4 ÷ .12	30. 72.390 ÷ 1.5
7. 3505.6 ÷ .7	19. 30.020 ÷ .05	31. .03015 ÷ .09
8. .144 ÷ .08	20. 119.7 ÷ .21	32. .00175 ÷ .35
9. 244.2 ÷ .03	21. 3.888 ÷ .9	33. .1896 ÷ .003
10. 56.98 ÷ .07	22. .014580 ÷ .04	34. .24 ÷ .0002
11. .03752 ÷ .07	23. 307.7580 ÷ .33	35. 11.2 ÷ .007
12. .42 ÷ .0006	24. .09872 ÷ .002	36. 14.40 ÷ .0012

12-7   If the Divisor Is Greater Than the Dividend

Example:

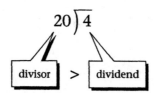

We cannot divide 4 by 20. But using decimals, we can. Remember from Chapter 11:

$$4 = 4.0 = 4.00 = 4.000 \quad \text{etc.}$$

We can write any integer, or whole number, as a decimal. We just write a decimal point to the right of the whole number and as many zeros as needed:

$$24 = 24.0 = 24.00 = 24.000 = 24.0000 \quad \text{etc.}$$

Returning to our problem: 20⟌4

   1. Write 4 as a decimal: 4 = 4.0

   We now have: 20⟌4.0

2. Now we can divide:

$$\begin{array}{r} .2 \\ 20\overline{)4{.}0} \\ \underline{-4\,0} \\ 0 \end{array}$$

Example:

$$40\overline{)2}$$

1. Write the dividend as a decimal. We can write it as 2.0 or 2.00. Which one?

$$40\overline{)2{.}0} \qquad \begin{array}{r} .05 \\ 40\overline{)2{.}00} \end{array}$$

We still cannot divide because 40 is greater than 20.

But we *can* divide 200 by 40. The answer is .05. We need to write in two zeros.

If the divisor is *much larger* than the dividend, you may need to write in *more* than one zero.

Example:

$$300\overline{).36}$$

1. Rewrite the decimal point above ↑ to the quotient:

$$300\overline{)\overset{.}{\uparrow}36}$$

We cannot divide 36 by 300.

2. Since .36 = .360, we can write one zero to the right of 6. Now divide:

$$\begin{array}{r} .001 \\ 300\overline{)\overset{}{\uparrow}360} \\ \underline{-300} \\ 60 \\ \uparrow \end{array}$$

There is a remainder of 60.

3. Write in one more zero in the dividend and continue to divide:

$$\begin{array}{r} .0012 \\ 300\overline{).3600} \\ -\ 300 \\ \hline 600 \\ -\ 600 \\ \hline 0 \end{array}$$

When there is a *remainder*, we need to write in *more* zeros in the dividend and continue to divide and write in zeros until there is no remainder.

BE CAREFUL!

In the example above, you *must* write in zeros after the decimal point in the quotient:

$$\begin{array}{r} .0012 \\ 300\overline{).3600} \end{array} \qquad \begin{array}{r} .\ \ 12 \\ 300\overline{).3600} \end{array}$$

        correct   not correct

$$.0012 \neq .\ \ 12$$

Exercise 12-J

Divide the following.

1. $4 \div 20$	13. $1 \div 8$	25. $3.445 \div 65$
2. $6 \div 8$	14. $10.5 \div 700$	26. $.209 \div 11$
3. $3 \div 4$	15. $22.95 \div 850$	27. $.5456 \div 62$
4. $3 \div 6$	16. $1.6 \div 20$	28. $.66 \div 200$
5. $3 \div 5$	17. $.3 \div 25$	29. $2 \div 5$
6. $7 \div 8$	18. $.475 \div 50$	30. $1 \div 25$
7. $2 \div 8$	19. $4.5 \div 60$	31. $.1 \div 8$
8. $.12 \div 8$	20. $1.64 \div 20$	32. $.1 \div 25$
9. $.2 \div 5$	21. $4 \div 50$	33. $3 \div 400$
10. $10 \div 50$	22. $1.4 \div 400$	34. $1 \div 250$
11. $4.8 \div 800$	23. $22.5 \div 45$	35. $.4 \div 20$
12. $.3 \div 4$	24. $.054 \div 30$	36. $.1 \div 5$

Divide the following.

1. 6.39 ÷ 3
2. 72.4 ÷ .2
3. 75.85 ÷ 5
4. 33 ÷ .11
5. .3 ÷ 5
6. 2 ÷ .005
7. 86.48 ÷ 8
8. .5266 ÷ 4
9. 3 ÷ 4000
10. .665 ÷.025

11. 943.06 ÷ 4
12. .1 ÷ 80
13. .00350 ÷ .50
14. 672.5 ÷ .05
15. 2.8 ÷ 800
16. 20 ÷ 100
17. 2.8 ÷ .14
18. 6493 ÷ .004
19. 1 ÷ 40
20. 9.0 ÷ 120

21. 7 ÷ 8
22. 9.9456 ÷ 56
23. .675 ÷ 30
24. 24 ÷ .0008
25. .02916 ÷ .08
26. 7.776 ÷ .18
27. 12 ÷ 16
28. .418 ÷ 22
29. 1.32 ÷ 400
30. 84 ÷ 1.20

12-8 Problem Solving with Decimals

Example:

Joel bought 6 pounds of chicken for $7.50. David bought 4 pounds of turkey for $5.20. Which is the **better buy?**

First, we must find the cost *per pound* (for 1 pound) of both the chicken and the turkey. Then we compare the prices. To find the cost *per pound*, divide the price by the total pounds:

chicken:
$$
\begin{array}{r}
1.25 \\
6 \overline{)\ 7.50} \\
-6 \\
\hline
1\,5 \\
-1\,2 \\
\hline
30 \\
-30 \\
\hline
0
\end{array}
$$

turkey:
$$
\begin{array}{r}
1.30 \\
4 \overline{)\ 5.20} \\
-4 \\
\hline
1\,2 \\
-1\,2 \\
\hline
00 \\
-0 \\
\hline
0
\end{array}
$$

The *better buy* is the chicken, at $1.25 a pound.

Marta and Yuri need to go shopping for the Math Club party. Help them decide which items are the *better buys*.

1. Marta and Yuri will buy sodas for the party. Super Cooler sodas are 8 cans for $3.36. Just Right sodas are 6 cans for $2.46.
   a. How much are Super Cooler sodas *per can*?
   b. How much are Just Right sodas *per can*?
   c. Which is the *better buy*?

2. Marta wants to buy Blue Star potato chips for 3 bags for $2.67. Yuri wants to buy Red Star potato chips for 5 bags for $4.55.
   a. How much are Blue Star potato chips *per bag*?
   b. How much are Red Star potato chips *per bag*?
   c. Which is the *better buy*?

3. Chocolate chip cookies are $2.88 a dozen. Peanut butter cookies are $1.92 for 8.
   a. How much is one chocolate chip cookie?
   b. How much is one peanut butter cookie?
   c. Which is the *better buy*?

4. Candy bars cost $.40 each. How many bars can the girls buy for $8?

5. Peanuts cost $.89 a bag. How many bags can Marta and Yuri buy for $4.45?

6. There are 20 students in the Math Club. Marta and Yuri will buy 3 pounds of oranges. How many pounds will each student have to eat?

12-9 Average or Mean

Example:

On Monday, the temperature was 90 degrees. On Tuesday, the temperature was 70 degrees. What was the average or mean temperature for both days?

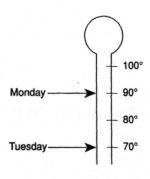

Monday ——→ 100°
90°
80°
Tuesday ——→ 70°

The *average*, or *mean*, is the *middle* number in a group of numbers. To find the average, or mean:

1. Add the numbers together.
2. Divide the sum by the number of *addends*.

$$70° + 90° = 160°$$

2 addends

$$160° \div 2 = 80°$$

Example:

Here are the math test scores for five students:

Becky	18
Jaimie	17
Wilson	20
Hanh	15
Henry	10

What is the **average**, *or* **mean** *score?*

$$18 + 17 + 20 + 15 + 10 = 80$$

5 addends

$$80 \div 5 = 16$$

The *average*, or *mean*, score is 16.

Exercise 12-M

Find the average, or mean, for each of the following.

1. Mark weighs 135.7 pounds, Teresa weighs 105.73 pounds, Violet weighs 127.33 pounds, and Harry weighs 119 pounds. What is the mean weight of all four people?

2. In May, apples were $.79 per pound. In June, apples were $1.23 per pound, and in July, apples cost $1.19 per pound. What was the average cost of apples for all 3 months?

3. Here are Mr. Contini's telephone bills for the year:

January	$23.19	July	$32.95
February	$16.45	August	$45.16
March	$30.20	September	$24.59
April	$22.74	October	$27.33
May	$19.50	November	$21.00
June	$18.48	December	$25.47

a. What was his average bill for January through June?
b. What was his average bill for the first 3 months?
c. What was his average bill for the last 3 months?
d. What was his average bill for the whole year? Round your answer to the nearest cent (hundredths' place).

4. In the Radar Corporation, 4 employees earn $35,000 a year, 2 employees earn $53,000 a year, and 17 employees earn $28,000 a year. What is the mean salary of the employees? Round your answer to the nearest whole number (ones' place).

Exercise 12-N

Use the *inverse operations* to find the missing numbers.

1. ___ ÷ .2 = 3.4
2. ___ ÷ .122 = 4.5
3. .5 × ___ = 25.5
4. ___ × .3 = 9.9
5. ___ ÷ 4.5 = 12.6
6. .9 × ___ = .81

7. ___ ÷ .98 = 8.54
8. ___ ÷ .8 = 12.34
9. ___ × .10 = 3.0
10. ___ ÷ .87 = 54.4
11. ___ ÷ .91 = 12.4
12. .7 × ___ = .42

13. .002 × ___ = 26
14. ___ ÷ .65 = 90
15. .004 × ___ = .56
16. 1.2 × ___ = .36
17. .005 × ___ = 3.5
18. ___ ÷ 6.55 = .12

12-10 Dividing Decimals by Multiples of Ten

We learned that to multiply decimals by *multiples of ten*, we move the decimal point to the *right*. To divide decimals by multiples of ten, we move the decimal point to the *left*.

Example:

$$436.2 \div 100 = 4.362$$

2 zeros

Move the point 2 places ←

$$25467.1 \div 10^5 = .254671$$

5 zeros

Move the point 5 places ←

Example:

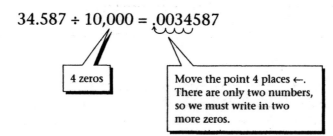

$$34.587 \div 10{,}000 = .0034587$$

4 zeros

Move the point 4 places ←.
There are only two numbers,
so we must write in two
more zeros.

Exercise 12-O

Divide the decimals by moving the decimal point.

1. $14.2 \div 10$
2. $7.11 \div 100$
3. $.673 \div 1{,}000$
4. $143.22 \div 100$
5. $7 \div 1{,}000$
6. $19 \div 10$
7. $376 \div 100$
8. $44.4 \div 10$
9. $444 \div 100$
10. $.444 \div 10$
11. $3294.11 \div 10{,}000$
12. $7463.4 \div 10$
13. $2.1 \div 1{,}000$
14. $111.4 \div 100$
15. $14.31 \div 10{,}000$
16. $5342 \div 1{,}000$
17. $1.433 \div 100$
18. $9 \div 10{,}000$
19. $3 \div 100$
20. $2 \div 10{,}000$

Exercise 12-P

Divide.

1. $43.5 \div 10^2$
2. $.1254 \div 10^3$
3. $365.66 \div 10^3$
4. $354.99 \div 10^4$
5. $.12938 \div 10^3$
6. $1543.66 \div 10^5$
7. $3546 \div 10^3$
8. $2435.1 \div 10^7$
9. $34.445 \div 10^2$
10. $34.777 \div 10^1$
11. $9{,}887.1 \div 10^0$
12. $9{,}857 \div 10^4$
13. $.88675 \div 10^7$
14. $.12 \div 10^5$

15. $95{,}744.32 \div 10^3$

16. $.7756 \div 10^0$

17. $34.44 \div 10^2$

18. $2{,}300 \div 10^2$

19. $1{,}000 \div 10^3$

20. $10{,}000 \div 10^4$

LET'S TALK ABOUT ...

1. increase
2. decrease
3. per pound
4. average
5. mean
6. take-home pay

Multiply the following.

1. 5.46×4
2. $.457 \times 32$
3. $7.22 \times .01$
4. $.001 \times .45$
5. 854.3×2.3
6. $1.26 \times .34$
7. $.945 \times .12$
8. $487.44 \times .002$
9. 54.667×12.3

Divide the following.

10. $4.24 \div 2$
11. $12.4 \div .2$
12. $15.50 \div .05$
13. $4 \div .002$
14. $2 \div 2000$
15. $.4032 \div .336$
16. $.3 \div 50$
17. $30 \div 600$
18. $.00856 \div .214$

Multiply or divide.

19. 5.48×10^2
20. 6.334×10^4
21. $7834.3 \div 10^3$
22. $.1255 \div 10^2$
23. $.3665 \times 10^6$
24. 1543.2×10^4
25. $9.567 \div 10^3$
26. $.213 \div 10^0$
27. 34.992×10^5

Solve the following.

28. Raul spends $11.70 on gasoline each month. How much does he spend in 1 year?

29. Maggie bought 1.75 pounds of chocolate. Chocolate cost $1.20 a pound. How much did she pay for the chocolate?

30. Casey went shopping. She bought 2.5 pounds of apples for $1.25. How much did she pay *per pound*?

31. Maurice received $279.27 for 32.5 hours of work last month. How much does he earn per *hour*?

32. For the month of January, Chan received four paychecks:

Week 1	$100.00
Week 2	$93.75
Week 3	$112.50
Week 4	$106.25

What is his *average* weekly pay? (Round to the nearest cent.)

Unit 4 Vocabulary Words

1. Bill — Paper money, as in dollars.

2. Cent — The word we use in expressing coins (six cents).

3. Coin — Nonpaper money, as in penny, nickel, dime, etc.

4. Decimals — Quantities written with a number and a decimal point (3.45, for example).

5. Dime — A coin with a value of ten cents ($.10).

6. Dollar — A bill with the value of $1.00.

7. Half-Dollar — A coin with a value of fifty cents ($ .50).

8. Hundredths' Place — In the decimal .64, the digit 4 is in the hundredths' place.

9. Hundred Thousandths' Place — In the decimal .64578, the digit 8 is in the hundred thousandths' place.

10. Millionths' Place — In the decimal .645789, the digit 9 is in the millionths' place.

11. Nickel — A coin with a value of five cents ($.05).

12. Penny — A coin with a value of one cent ($.01).

13. Quarter — A coin with a value of twenty-five cents ($ .25).

14. Tenths' Place — In the decimal .6, the digit 6 is in the tenths' place.

15. Ten Thousandths' Place — In the decimal .6457, the digit 7 is in the ten thousandths' place.

16. Thousandths' Place — In the decimal .645, the digit 5 is in the thousandths' place.

APPENDIX

Listening Scripts

Unit 1 Chapter 1

LISTEN! READING AND SAYING NUMBERS

Read the numbers aloud, slowly and clearly. Repeat once.

1. two hundred ninety
2. fourteen
3. three hundred fifteen
4. nine hundred ninety
5. three thousand one hundred-fifty
6. four hundred twenty-six thousand, thirteen
7. six million, one hundred ninety thousand, two hundred sixty
8. one hundred seven thousand, thirty
9. five million, three hundred thousand
10. eight million, six thousand, ninety-five
11. six hundred thousand, nine
12. fourteen million, fifty-five

Exercise 1-B

Have students practice saying the numbers aloud, one by one, in Exercise 1-B on page 6. Correct pronunciation as needed. Pay special attention to the following pairs of numbers:

30 and 13 *(thirty and thirteen)*	70 and 17
40 and 14	80 and 18
50 and 15	90 and 19
60 and 16	55 and 65

(If necessary, exaggerate the syllables which receive the accent)

SPEAKING UP! READING AND SAYING NUMBERS

Students will look at the program card on page 15 to answer the questions below. Read the questions aloud, slowly and clearly. Repeat once. As students answer, correct pronunciation of numbers:

1. Whose program card is this?
2. How many classes does Ricky have?
3. What period does Ricky have art?
4. On what floor does Ricky study history?
5. Who is Ricky's third period teacher?
6. What period does Ricky have Algebra?
7. On what floor does Ricky study Algebra?
8. On what day in October was Ricky born?
9. What grade is Ricky in?
10. What class does Ricky have fourth period?
11. In what year was Ricky born?
12. What period does Ricky have physical education?
13. What is the date on the program card?
14. In what room does Ricky study English?
15. Where does Kato teach art?

LISTEN!

Read the questions and/or statements aloud, slowly and clearly. Repeat once. Students will write the letter next to the correct answer.

1. How many numbers are there on a number line?
2. What word means the same as estimate?
3. A round number has one or more _____ as the end digits.
4. The number two hundred six has how many digits?
5. Another word for largest is _____.
6. In the number 15, what is the place name of the digit 5?
7. Another word for least is _____.
8. A number line has no beginning and no _____.
9. The number 2 is a cardinal number and the number 2nd is an _____.
10. Cardinal numbers tell how many and ordinal numbers tell _____.

LISTEN!

Read the statements aloud, slowly and clearly. Repeat once. Students will write the letter next to the statement they hear.

1. four squared
2. seventeen is less than thirty-two
3. sixteen is greater than twelve
4. five times thirty
5. eleven is equal to m
6. fourteen is less than t
7. x squared plus y cubed
8. eight squared plus two cubed
9. r divided by s
10. three squared

11. ten to the fifth power minus one hundred squared
12. *b* to the fourth power
13. negative six is greater than negative nine
14. *m* cubed is greater than *m* squared
15. negative forty is less than negative fourteen
16. six to the zero power
17. three to the fourth power is equal to eighty-one
18. ten to the sixth power

LISTEN!

Read the decimals aloud, slowly and clearly. Repeat once. Students will write the letter next to the decimal they hear.

1. four and three tenths
2. seventy-four hundredths
3. one and ninety hundredths
4. six hundred thirteen thousandths
5. three and forty hundredths
6. one hundredth
7. seven and six thousandths
8. fifteen hundredths
9. forty-five and nine tenths
10. five hundred seven thousandths